OFFICIAL SQA PAST PAPERS WITH ANSWERS

STANDARD GRADE | CREDIT

FRENCH
2006-2010

2006 EXAM – page 3
Credit Level Reading 2006
Credit Level Listening Transcript 2006
Credit Level Listening 2006

2007 EXAM – page 21
Credit Level Reading 2007
Credit Level Listening Transcript 2007
Credit Level Listening 2007

2008 EXAM – page 39
Credit Level Reading 2008
Credit Level Listening Transcript 2008
Credit Level Listening 2008

2009 EXAM – page 55
Credit Level Reading 2009
Credit Level Listening Transcript 2009
Credit Level Listening 2009

2010 EXAM – page 73
Credit Level Reading 2010
Credit Level Listening Transcript 2010
Credit Level Listening 2010

First exam published in 2006.
Published by Bright Red Publishing Ltd, 6 Stafford Street, Edinburgh EH3 7AU
tel: 0131 220 5804 fax: 0131 220 6710 info@brightredpublishing.co.uk www.brightredpublishing.co.uk

ISBN 978-1-84948-090-1

A CIP Catalogue record for this book is available from the British Library.

Bright Red Publishing is grateful to the copyright holders, as credited on the final page of the book, for permission to use their material. Every effort has been made to trace the copyright holders and to obtain their permission for the use of copyright material. Bright Red Publishing will be happy to receive information allowing us to rectify any error or omission in future editions.

STANDARD GRADE | CREDIT

2006

[BLANK PAGE]

FOR OFFICIAL USE

C

Total

1000/403

NATIONAL
QUALIFICATIONS
2006

TUESDAY, 9 MAY
11.10 AM – 12.10 PM

FRENCH
STANDARD GRADE
Credit Level
Reading

Fill in these boxes and read what is printed below.

Full name of centre

Town

Forename(s)

Surname

Date of birth
Day Month Year

Scottish candidate number

Number of seat

When you are told to do so, open your paper and write your answers **in English** in the spaces provided.

You may use a French dictionary.

Before leaving the examination room you must give this book to the invigilator. If you do not, you may lose all the marks for this paper.

SCOTTISH
QUALIFICATIONS
AUTHORITY

PB 1000/403 6/23970

©

Marks

You are reading a French magazine.

1. A girl has written to the advice page of the magazine with some concerns about smoking.

Chère Anne!

Beaucoup de mes amies fument déjà, et elles n'arrêtent pas de me dire que fumer c'est extra, et que je devrais essayer.

J'ai peur qu'elles ne me parlent plus si je refuse de fumer avec elles. Que dois-je faire?

Bernadette, 13 ans.

Complete the sentences.

(a) Bernadette's friends say that smoking is _____   2

and that she _____ .

(b) If Bernadette refuses, she is afraid that her friends _____   1

_____ .

Marks

2. The editor of the magazine has answered Bernadette's letter.

Fumer ou ne pas fumer, c'est une décision pour chaque individu.

Il faut savoir que . . .

. . . presque la moitié des jeunes Français âgés de 15 à 24 ans fument.

. . . les filles qui fument sont de plus en plus nombreuses et elles sont plus jeunes quand elles commencent à fumer.

Dans quelques années, tes copines auront la mauvaise haleine et les doigts jaunes – sans parler de maladies bien plus graves. En expliquant tout ça à tes copines, tu peux leur montrer que tu as de très bonnes raisons pour dire "non" à la cigarette.

Tu sais que, depuis le début de l'année, les médias refusent de donner une image positive des fumeurs. Au contraire ils informent le public des dangers du tabac pour la santé.

(*a*) What statistic is given about French people between the ages of 15 and 24?   1

_____

(*b*) What information is given about girls? Mention any **one** thing.   1

_____

_____

(*c*) What problems will Bernadette's friends have in a few years? Mention any **two** things.   2

_____

_____

(*d*) How are the media helping in the campaign against smoking? Mention any **one** thing.   1

_____

[Turn over

Marks

3.   You come across an article about an environmental problem.

La France sous les déchets

Vous avez vu tous les emballages qu'on jette à la poubelle quand on revient du supermarché? La société est devenue trop gourmande en emballage. En 1975 un Français produisait 500g d'ordures ménagères par jour. Aujourd'hui il en produit un kilo.

Le Ministre de l'Ecologie lance un plan d'action. Elle demande aux consommateurs de faire des efforts pour utiliser moins d'emballages. Comme ça on va gaspiller moins de papier.

Une grande campagne de publicité va encourager les Français à acheter des produits qui respectent l'environnement et à réutiliser les sacs plastiques.

(*a*)   What has doubled since 1975?   **1**

_____

_____

(*b*)   (i)   What does the Minister for the Environment want people to do?   **2**

_____

(ii)   Why?

_____

(*c*)   What is the purpose of the publicity campaign? Mention **two** things.   **2**

_____

_____

Marks

4.   You read an article about the work of a pharmacist.

Marcel, 52 ans, pharmacien dans un village du Haut-Rhin.

Je voulais faire quelque chose dans le domaine des sciences et au lycée
j'aimais la biochimie et la physique, donc j'ai étudié la pharmacologie à
l'université.

Les pharmaciens ont six ans d'étude après le bac, donc ils finissent leurs
études assez tard, à l'âge de 23 ans ou plus. Deux pharmaciens sur trois
travaillent dans les pharmacies et les autres dans les laboratoires des
hôpitaux et chez les fabricants de médicaments.

Pour faire ce métier, il faut s'intéresser aux gens et s'entendre bien avec ses
clients. Mes clients me racontent leurs problèmes de santé et je leur
explique les ordonnances.

(*a*)   Why did Marcel choose to study pharmacy? Mention any **one** thing.   1

_____

_____

(*b*)   What does he say about becoming a pharmacist? Mention any **one** thing.   1

_____

_____

(*c*)   Apart from pharmacies, where do most pharmacists work? Mention **two**
things.   2

_____

_____

(*d*)   What does he say about his job? Mention any **two** things.   2

_____

_____

[Turn over

Marks

5. You read an article in which young French people discuss whether machines are good or bad for society.

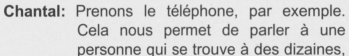

Les machines nous apportent des biens. Oui! Mais ......

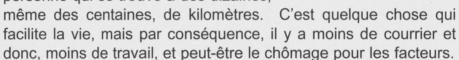

Chantal: Prenons le téléphone, par exemple. Cela nous permet de parler à une personne qui se trouve à des dizaines, même des centaines, de kilomètres. C'est quelque chose qui facilite la vie, mais par conséquence, il y a moins de courrier et donc, moins de travail, et peut-être le chômage pour les facteurs.

Mathieu: Plus on a de machines, plus on a de besoins. Par exemple, on a inventé le portable. Mais, pour les faire fonctionner, on a besoin de chargeurs et d'un réseau.

Thierry: Et maintenant il y a les ordinateurs. Dans l'avenir, les ordinateurs feront tout le travail des hommes, mais les gens ne vont pas s'ennuyer. Au lieu de travailler, ils pourront consacrer tout leur temps à s'amuser.

(a) According to Chantal the telephone has been a useful invention. But, what are the disadvantages? Mention any **two** things.

2

_____

_____

(b) What invention does Mathieu talk about?

1

_____

(c) Why is it of little use on its own?

1

_____

(d) What does Thierry say about the effect of computers? Mention **three** things.

3

_____

_____

[END OF QUESTION PAPER] **Total (26)**

C

1000/409

NATIONAL
QUALIFICATIONS
2006

TUESDAY, 9 MAY
2.30 PM – 3.00 PM
(APPROX)

FRENCH
STANDARD GRADE
Credit Level
Listening Transcript

This paper must not be seen by any candidate.

The material overleaf is provided for use in an emergency only (eg the recording or equipment proving faulty) or where permission has been given in advance by SQA for the material to be read to candidates with additional support needs. The material must be read exactly as printed.

SCOTTISH
QUALIFICATIONS
AUTHORITY

©

Transcript—Credit Level

Instructions to reader(s):

For each item, read the English **once,** then read the French **three times**, with an interval of 5 seconds between the readings. On completion of the third reading, pause for the length of time indicated in brackets after each item, to allow the candidates to write their answers.

Where special arrangements have been agreed in advance to allow the reading of the material, those sections marked **(f)** should be read by a female speaker and those marked **(m)** by a male: those sections marked **(t)** should be read by the teacher.

(t) You are spending your holidays with your family in a hotel in France.

(m) or (f)   **Tu passes les vacances avec ta famille dans un hôtel en France.**

(t) Question number one.

You meet a French boy called Georges who introduces you to his twin sister, Nicole. What does he say?

(m)   **Voici ma soeur, Nicole. Nous sommes jumeaux. Heureusement, nous nous entendons très bien. J'ai de très bons rapports avec elle.**

(40 seconds)

(t) Question number two.

Georges' mother tells you about their holidays. What does she say? Mention any **two** things.

(f)   **En général, on passe seulement une semaine ici en juillet parce que mon mari doit travailler. Pour nous, les vacances principales sont en hiver. Nous passons une quinzaine à faire du ski en Suisse.**

(40 seconds)

(t) Question number three.

She then explains what there is to do in the area. What does she say? Mention any **two** things.

(f)   **Passer les vacances ici, ça me plaît beaucoup. Il y a tant de choses à faire pour les jeunes. Il y a un parc d'attractions pas loin d'ici. Et en plus, on peut faire de l'équitation.**

(40 seconds)

(t) Question number four.

Georges talks about his sporting activities. What does he tell you? Mention any **two** things.

(m)   **Moi, j'ai la chance d'être doué pour le sport. Je fais des sports d'équipe et des sports individuels. Au collège, je suis champion de natation.**

(40 seconds)

(t) **Question number five.**

What did he do during the Easter holidays? Mention any **two** things.

(m)   **Pendant les vacances de Pâques, j'ai travaillé dans un club pour les enfants âgés de cinq à dix ans. C'était une expérience formidable pour moi! J'ai passé toute la journée en plein air avec les enfants.**

(40 seconds)

(t) **Question number six.**

What does Georges say about his school subjects? What does he say about the kind of job he wants? Mention any **one** thing.

(m)   **Je ne suis pas fort en maths et en français. Être assis dans un bureau ne m'intéresse pas du tout. Je sais que je dois trouver un métier où je serai tout le temps actif.**

(40 seconds)

(t) **Question number seven.**

Nicole tells you she wants to be a librarian. What does she say about her childhood which shows her interest in books? Mention **two** things.

(f)   **Depuis très longtemps, je veux devenir bibliothécaire. Quand j'étais enfant, je lisais avec enthousiasme des livres de toutes sortes. Quelquefois, j'oubliais de venir manger avec la famille parce que je voulais finir mon livre.**

(40 seconds)

(t) **Question number eight.**

What has Nicole done to prepare herself for the job of librarian? Mention **two** things.

(f)   **Au mois de juillet, j'ai travaillé dans la bibliothèque municipale de notre ville. J'ai remplacé un bibliothécaire qui était en vacances. C'était intéressant et très utile pour moi.**

(40 seconds)

(t) **Question number nine.**

Libraries are not just for lending books. For what other reasons do people go there? Mention **two** things.

(f)   **Tu sais, aujourd'hui, le travail de bibliothécaire ne consiste pas seulement à distribuer les livres. Dans presque toutes les bibliothèques, on trouve des ordinateurs et beaucoup de gens viennent chercher des informations sur Internet. Et il y a aussi des étudiants qui doivent faire des recherches pour préparer leurs examens.**

(40 seconds)

[Turn over for Questions 10 to 13 on *Page four*

(t) Question number ten.

Their father talks about his first job helping his uncle. What did his uncle do for a living? How did he help him?

(m)   **Mon oncle avait une petite ferme où il cultivait des fruits et des légumes. A l'âge de quinze ans, je l'aidais à transporter les produits au marché tous les samedi matins.**

(*40 seconds*)

(t) Question number eleven.

What does Nicole say about her mother? She sometimes has problems with her dad. Why? Mention any **one** thing.

(f)   **Dans l'ensemble, ma mère me traite comme une adulte mais quelquefois j'ai des problèmes avec mon père. Il est protecteur quand je veux sortir. Il ne comprend pas que je ne suis plus une enfant.**

(*40 seconds*)

(t) Question number twelve.

Their mother also talks about what happens when young people go to university. What does she say? Mention any **two** things.

(f)   **Quand les jeunes vont à l'université ils veulent être indépendants, bien sûr! Mais ils sont souvent influencés par les autres et il y a toujours la tentation de prendre de la drogue ou de trop boire.**

(*40 seconds*)

(t) Question number thirteen.

What does their father say about Nicole and Georges and the work they will do? Mention any **two** things.

(m)   **Nicole et Georges, ils sont très différents l'un de l'autre. Mais ce qu'ils feront dans la vie ne m'inquiète pas. L'important, c'est qu'ils trouvent un métier où ils sont heureux, un emploi qui leur plaît.**

(*40 seconds*)

(t) End of test.

Now look over your answers.

[*END OF TRANSCRIPT*]

FOR OFFICIAL USE

C

Total Marks

1000/408

NATIONAL
QUALIFICATIONS
2006

TUESDAY, 9 MAY
2.30 PM – 3.00 PM
(APPROX)

FRENCH
STANDARD GRADE
Credit Level
Listening

Fill in these boxes and read what is printed below.

Full name of centre

Town

Forename(s)

Surname

Date of birth
Day Month Year

Scottish candidate number

Number of seat

When you are told to do so, open your paper.

You will hear a number of short items in French. You will hear each item three times, then you will have time to write your answer.

Write your answers, **in English**, in this book, in the appropriate spaces.

You may take notes as you are listening to the French, but only in this paper.

You may **not** use a French dictionary.

You are not allowed to leave the examination room until the end of the test.

Before leaving the examination room you must give this book to the invigilator. If you do not, you may lose all the marks for this paper.

SCOTTISH
QUALIFICATIONS
AUTHORITY

©

Marks

You are spending your holidays with your family in a hotel in France.

Tu passes les vacances avec ta famille dans un hôtel en France.

1. You meet a French boy called Georges who introduces you to his twin sister, Nicole. What does he say?

1

_____

_____

*   *   *   *   *

2. Georges' mother tells you about their holidays.   What does she say? Mention any **two** things.

2

_____

_____

*   *   *   *   *

3. She then explains what there is to do in the area. What does she say? Mention any **two** things.

2

_____

_____

*   *   *   *   *

4. Georges talks about his sporting activities. What does he tell you? Mention any **two** things.

2

_____

_____

*   *   *   *   *

Marks

5. What did he do during the Easter holidays? Mention any **two** things.

2

*   *   *   *   *

6. (*a*)   What does Georges say about his school subjects?

1

    (*b*)   What does he say about the kind of job he wants? Mention any **one** thing.

1

*   *   *   *   *

7. Nicole tells you she wants to be a librarian. What does she say about her childhood which shows her interest in books? Mention **two** things.

2

*   *   *   *   *

8. What has Nicole done to prepare herself for the job of librarian? Mention **two** things.

2

*   *   *   *   *

[Turn over

Marks

9. Libraries are not just for lending books. For what other reasons do people go there? Mention **two** things.

_____

_____

2

*   *   *   *   *

10. Their father talks about his first job helping his uncle.

    (*a*)   What did his uncle do for a living?

    _____

    1

    (*b*)   How did he help him?

    _____

    1

*   *   *   *   *

11. (*a*)   What does Nicole say about her mother?

    _____

    1

    (*b*)   She sometimes has problems with her dad. Why? Mention any **one** thing.

    _____

    1

*   *   *   *   *

12. Their mother also talks about what happens when young people go to university. What does she say? Mention any **two** things.

    _____

    _____

    2

*   *   *   *   *

Marks

13. What does their father say about Nicole and Georges and the work they will do? Mention any **two** things.

2

_____

_____

*   *   *   *   *

Total (25)

[*END OF QUESTION PAPER*]

[BLANK PAGE]

STANDARD GRADE | CREDIT

2007

[BLANK PAGE]

FOR OFFICIAL USE

C

Total

1000/403

NATIONAL
QUALIFICATIONS
2007

WEDNESDAY, 9 MAY
11.10 AM – 12.10 PM

FRENCH
STANDARD GRADE
Credit Level
Reading

Fill in these boxes and read what is printed below.

Full name of centre

Town

Forename(s)

Surname

Date of birth
Day Month Year   Scottish candidate number   Number of seat

When you are told to do so, open your paper and write your answers **in English** in the spaces provided.

You may use a French dictionary.

Before leaving the examination room you must give this book to the invigilator. If you do not, you may lose all the marks for this paper.

SCOTTISH
QUALIFICATIONS
AUTHORITY

Marks

1. Some young French people have written to a website with their views on being an only child.

Être enfant unique—avantage ou inconvénient?

Moi, je suis fille unique et ce n'est pas du tout un inconvénient. Mais, on a des problèmes familiaux quand même.

Je crois que je reçois plus d'attention de mes parents parce que je suis seule, mais mes parents me mettent aussi beaucoup de pression avec mes études.

On ne devrait pas comparer la vie seule à la vie avec des frères et des soeurs parce qu'on ne peut rien changer.

Marion (Rouen)

Je suis enfant unique et cela me va très bien. Je ne peux pas m'imaginer avec un frère ou une soeur. Je ne me sens pas seul, parce que je ne manque pas d'amis au collège.

Si j'avais un frère, il faudrait tout partager—les bonbons, les cadeaux, l'argent de poche, peut-être ma chambre. Quelle horreur!

Thierry (Boulogne)

(a) According to Marion, what is the advantage of being an only child?   1

_____

(b) What disadvantage is there for her?   1

_____

(c) Why does she think you should not compare being an only child with having brothers and sisters?   1

_____

(d) Thierry does not feel lonely. Why?   1

_____

(e) Why would he not like to have a brother?   1

_____

Marks

2. This article gives advice to parents who are worried about children who have an untidy room.

Quel bazar* dans la chambre!

Pour éduquer un enfant à garder de l'ordre dans sa chambre, il faut commencer tôt.

A partir de trois ans, on peut demander à l'enfant de mettre son nounours sur une chaise et de ramasser ses jouets. Ne dites jamais: "Range ta chambre", parce que c'est une idée que l'enfant est incapable de comprendre. Pour un enfant de sept à huit ans on peut dire: "Ne laisse pas traîner tes affaires par terre" et "Rapporte les verres et les assiettes sales à la cuisine".

*bazar = a mess

(a) To teach a child to keep his room in order, what must a parent do?   **1**

_____

(b) What can a three-year old be asked to do? Mention **two** things.   **2**

_____

_____

(c) What should parents never say to a three-year old?   **1**

_____

(d) What reason is given for this?   **1**

_____

(e) What can a parent ask a seven or eight-year old child to do? Mention **two** things.   **2**

_____

_____

[Turn over

Marks

3.   The article about bringing up children continues.

A partir de douze ans, l'enfant considère sa chambre comme son espace personnel. Donc, les parents doivent prendre l'habitude de frapper avant d'entrer.

Pour les adolescents, il faut leur faire comprendre que la chambre fait partie de la maison. Donc, ils n'ont pas le droit de peindre les murs sans la permission de parents.

En ce qui concerne la musique, on ne doit pas accepter qu'ils jouent du "Rap" très fort sur le mp3, puisqu'il y a un risque de surdité.

On peut insister aussi sur la propreté. Les ados doivent passer l'aspirateur dans la chambre tous les quinze jours et ils doivent mettre leurs vêtements sales dans le panier à linge une fois par semaine.

(*a*) What should parents do when children reach the age of twelve?   1

_____

(*b*) If teenagers want to do something to their room what do they have to understand? Mention any **one** thing.   1

_____

(*c*) Why are parents entitled to insist that the volume of the mp3 player be kept down?   1

_____

(*d*) What should parents insist that young people do to keep their room tidy? Mention **two** things.   2

_____

_____

Marks

4. You then read an article about people who move to other countries.

POURQUOI QUITTER SON PAYS?

Un habitant du monde sur trente-cinq est immigré: une personne qui quitte son pays pour aller vivre dans un pays plus développé, pour trouver du travail et de meilleures conditions de vie. Mais beaucoup des pays qui les accueillent ne sont pas nécessairement riches. Souvent les entreprises et les usines sont en train de se développer et elles ont besoin d'employés.

Dans les pays d'accueil, ces immigrations peuvent poser des difficultés. Les immigrés s'installent parfois dans les régions où il y a moins de possibilités de travail et où il y a déjà beaucoup de chômage.

(*a*) Why does one person in 35 in the world leave his/her own country? Mention any **two** things.

2

_____

_____

(*b*) What information are we given about the countries people move to? Mention any **two** things.

2

_____

_____

(*c*) What difficulties can sometimes arise? Mention **two** things.

2

_____

_____

[Turn over

Marks

5. The article continues.

> Peut-être que ces immigrations pourraient être plus bénéfiques si elles étaient mieux organisées: par exemple, si on encourageait les immigrés à chercher des pays qui sont capables de leur offrir du travail. En ce moment, dans certains pays où ils vont, leur rêve de trouver du travail est souvent déçu. Par conséquent, ils n'ont pas de domicile fixe, pas de papiers et ils se retrouvent dans la pauvreté.

(*a*) It is suggested that immigration could be better organised. In what way?   **1**

_____

_____

(*b*) What are the consequences for people who do not find work? Mention any **two** things.   **2**

_____

_____

Total (26)

[END OF QUESTION PAPER]

C

1000/409

| NATIONAL QUALIFICATIONS 2007 | WEDNESDAY, 9 MAY 2.30 PM – 3.00 PM (APPROX) | **FRENCH STANDARD GRADE** Credit Level Listening Transcript |

This paper must not be seen by any candidate.

The material overleaf is provided for use in an emergency only (eg the recording or equipment proving faulty) or where permission has been given in advance by SQA for the material to be read to candidates with additional support needs. The material must be read exactly as printed.

SCOTTISH
QUALIFICATIONS
AUTHORITY

©

Transcript—Credit Level

> **Instructions to reader(s):**
>
> For each item, read the English **once,** then read the French **three times**, with an interval of 5 seconds between the readings. On completion of the third reading, pause for the length of time indicated in brackets after each item, to allow the candidates to write their answers.
>
> Where special arrangements have been agreed in advance to allow the reading of the material, those sections marked **(f)** should be read by a female speaker and those marked **(m)** by a male: those sections marked **(t)** should be read by the teacher.

(t) You are spending a holiday with Francine, your French pen-pal.

(m) or (f)   **Tu passes des vacances chez Francine, ta correspondante française.**

(t) Question number one.

Francine says you will be going to a club tonight. What does she say about the club? Complete the sentences.

(f)   **Ce soir, on va en boîte avec les copains. Le vendredi soir, c'est très populaire et il y a toujours beaucoup de monde. Mais si on arrive avant neuf heures, c'est gratuit pour les filles. Elles ne paient pas.**

(40 seconds)

(t) Question number two.

Francine talks about going out at night. What does she say? Complete the sentence.

(f)   **Je trouve que mes parents sont compréhensifs. Ils me permettent de sortir très tard si je leur dis où je vais, et avec qui.**

(40 seconds)

(t) Question number three.

Why is she not afraid when she is out late in town? Mention **two** things.

(f)   **Je n'ai pas peur quand je suis en ville après minuit, car je ne suis jamais seule; j'ai toujours mes copines avec moi. Et puis, j'ai mon portable dans ma poche.**

(40 seconds)

(t) Question number four.

Francine talks about her parents. What does she say about her mother? Mention any **one** thing. What sometimes causes arguments with her father?

(f)   **Je m'entends bien avec ma mère; je trouve qu'elle a des opinions et des attitudes très jeunes, très modernes. En général, ça va avec mon père aussi. Mais parfois, il y a des disputes qui sont provoquées par des questions d'argent.**

(40 seconds)

(t) Question number five.

What does Francine think about the pocket money she receives? What is her father's opinion?

(f) **Mes parents me donnent de l'argent de poche, mais cela ne me suffit pas. J'aimerais avoir un peu plus d'argent, mais mon père dit que je devrais trouver un travail le week-end.**

(40 seconds)

(t) Question number six.

Where does Francine hope to go in the summer? What will she find difficult?

(f) **En juillet, mes copines et moi, nous voulons partir dans un village de vacances à la montagne. C'est uniquement pour les adolescents. Bien sûr, je devrai faire des économies, et ça, c'est très difficile pour moi.**

(40 seconds)

(t) Question number seven.

What activities will be available during the day? Mention any **one** thing. What will they do in the evenings?

(m) or (f) **Pendant la journée, on pourra faire de l'escalade et des randonnées à cheval. Et, le soir, on va discuter des projets du lendemain.**

(40 seconds)

(t) Question number eight.

Why is Francine looking forward to the holiday so much?

(f) **Ce sera formidable parce que je vais passer un mois entier avec des jeunes de mon âge!**

(40 seconds)

(t) One evening you are listening to a French radio station. You hear an interview with Jacques Lambert, a French footballer who plays for a Scottish team.

(t) Question number nine.

What does Jacques say about his links with Scotland? Mention any **two** things.

(m) **Ça fait trois ans que j'habite en Ecosse et je viens d'acheter une nouvelle maison sur la côte ouest. Ma femme et moi, nous avons de très bons amis là-bas.**

(40 seconds)

[Turn over for Questions 10 to 13 on *Page four*

(t) Question number ten.

What difficulties did he have when he first arrived? Mention **two** things.

(m)   **Au début, je ne connaissais personne. Et, en plus, j'avais du mal à comprendre les Ecossais à cause de leur accent.**

(40 seconds)

(t) Question number eleven.

What does Jacques say about the players in his team? Mention any **one** thing. What do the coaches have to do?

(m)   **Dans notre équipe il y a des joueurs qui viennent de différents pays, et ils parlent plusieurs langues. Donc, quand les entraîneurs nous parlent en anglais, ils sont obligés de parler lentement.**

(40 seconds)

(t) Question number twelve.

What does he not like about living in Scotland? What problem does this cause?

(m)   **Je dois admettre que le climat m'énerve énormément. On ne sait jamais s'il va faire beau, donc on ne peut pas organiser facilement des activités en plein air.**

(40 seconds)

(t) Question number thirteen.

What was Jacques' childhood like? Mention any **one** thing. What is his life like now? Mention any **one** thing.

(m)   **Quand j'étais jeune, ma famille était assez pauvre. On habitait dans un tout petit appartement et on n'avait pas de voiture. Maintenant, je n'ai pas de problèmes financiers et j'ai la possibilité de voir le monde.**

(40 seconds)

(t) End of test.

Now look over your answers.

[END OF TRANSCRIPT]

C

FOR OFFICIAL USE

Total
Marks

1000/408

NATIONAL
QUALIFICATIONS
2007

WEDNESDAY, 9 MAY
2.30 PM – 3.00 PM
(APPROX)

FRENCH
STANDARD GRADE
Credit Level
Listening

Fill in these boxes and read what is printed below.

Full name of centre

Town

Forename(s)

Surname

Date of birth
Day Month Year   Scottish candidate number   Number of seat

When you are told to do so, open your paper.

You will hear a number of short items in French. You will hear each item three times, then you will have time to write your answer.

Write your answers, **in English**, in this book, in the appropriate spaces.

You may take notes as you are listening to the French, but only in this paper.

You may **not** use a French dictionary.

You are not allowed to leave the examination room until the end of the test.

Before leaving the examination room you must give this book to the invigilator. If you do not, you may lose all the marks for this paper.

SCOTTISH
QUALIFICATIONS
AUTHORITY

©

DO NO
WRITE
THIS
MARGI

Marks

You are spending a holiday with Francine, your French pen-pal.

Tu passes des vacances chez Francine, ta correspondante française.

1. Francine says you will be going to a club tonight. What does she say about the club? Complete the sentences.

      2

    On Fridays, the club _____

    _____ .

    Before nine o'clock _____ .

*   *   *   *   *

2. Francine talks about going out at night. What does she say? Complete the sentence.

      2

    Her parents let her go out late if _____

    _____ and _____ .

*   *   *   *   *

3. Why is she not afraid when she is out late in town? Mention **two** things.

      2

    _____

    _____

*   *   *   *   *

4. Francine talks about her parents.

    (*a*) What does she say about her mother? Mention any **one** thing.

      1

        _____

    (*b*) What sometimes causes arguments with her father?

      1

        _____

*   *   *   *   *

Marks

5. (a) What does Francine think about the pocket money she receives?   1

_____

(b) What is her father's opinion?   1

_____

*   *   *   *   *

6. (a) Where does Francine hope to go in the summer?   1

_____

(b) What will she find difficult?   1

_____

*   *   *   *   *

7. (a) What activities will be available during the day?   Mention any **one** thing.   1

_____

_____

(b) What will they do in the evenings?   1

_____

*   *   *   *   *

8. Why is Francine looking forward to the holiday so much?   1

_____

*   *   *   *   *

[Turn over

Marks

One evening you are listening to a French radio station. You hear an interview with Jacques Lambert, a French footballer who plays for a Scottish team.

9. What does Jacques say about his links with Scotland? Mention any **two** things.

2

_____

_____

*   *   *   *   *

10. What difficulties did he have when he first arrived? Mention **two** things.

2

_____

_____

*   *   *   *   *

11. (*a*) What does Jacques say about the players in his team? Mention any **one** thing.

1

_____

(*b*) What do the coaches have to do?

1

_____

*   *   *   *   *

12. (*a*) What does he not like about living in Scotland?

1

_____

(*b*) What problem does this cause?

1

_____

*   *   *   *   *

Marks

13. (*a*) What was Jacques' childhood like? Mention any **one** thing.

1

_____

(*b*) What is his life like now? Mention any **one** thing.

1

_____

*   *   *   *   *

Total (25)

[*END OF QUESTION PAPER*]

[BLANK PAGE]

2008

[BLANK PAGE]

FOR OFFICIAL USE

C

Total

1000/403

NATIONAL
QUALIFICATIONS
2008

TUESDAY, 13 MAY
11.10 AM – 12.10 PM

**FRENCH
STANDARD GRADE**
Credit Level
Reading

Fill in these boxes and read what is printed below.

Full name of centre

Town

Forename(s)

Surname

Date of birth
Day Month Year

Scottish candidate number

Number of seat

When you are told to do so, open your paper and write your answers **in English** in the spaces provided.

You may use a French dictionary.

Before leaving the examination room you must give this book to the invigilator. If you do not, you may lose all the marks for this paper.

Marks

1. You read an article in which some school pupils talk about friendships between boys and girls.

L'amitié filles—garçons

J'ai un petit copain, mais j'ai aussi beaucoup d'amis garçons. Quand j'ai des disputes avec mon copain, je peux parler à un autre garçon et cela m'aide à comprendre la mentalité masculine.

Valérie, 15 ans

Au collège, je fais partie d'une bande d'amis mixte. A la récréation nous sommes souvent ensemble et nous parlons de tout. Et nous faisons des sorties ensemble après les cours.

Thomas, 13 ans

Moi, je préfère discuter avec les filles individuellement. Elles rigolent tout le temps quand elles sont en groupe. Quand elles sont seules, par contre, on voit qu'elles ont leurs propres idées sur des sujets importants.

Marc, 15 ans

(*a*) What happens when Valérie has an argument with her boyfriend? Mention **two** things.

2

_____

_____

(*b*) What does Thomas say about his mixed group of friends? Mention any **two** things.

2

_____

_____

(*c*) Why does Marc prefer to speak to girls on an individual basis? Mention **two** things.

2

_____

_____

Marks

2. You then read one boy's ideas about how life might be in the future.

LA VIE DANS TRENTE ANS

La vie dans trente ans m'attire énormément car je pense que nous ne travaillerons plus. Tout le monde aura des robots qui feront notre boulot, bien sûr.

On se déplacera en voitures électriques ou bien je voyagerai en soucoupe volante dans l'espace et je parlerai avec des extra-terrestres qui seront, naturellement, mes meilleurs amis . . . Voilà.

Marc

(*a*) What does Marc say about work in 30 years time? Mention any **one** thing.

1

_____

(*b*) He goes on to describe a very different way of life in the future. What does he say? Mention any **two** things.

2

_____

_____

[Turn over

Marks

3. A girl then gives her ideas about the future.

> Mon rêve, c'est qu'en 2038 on aura trouvé des remèdes à tous les problèmes graves de nos jours. C'est-à-dire qu'il n'y aura plus de pauvreté ou de faim. Mais, à mon avis, ce n'est pas près d'arriver.
>
> Et voilà pourquoi. Je trouve que les gouvernements ne font pas assez pour résoudre les problèmes internationaux. Le pire c'est qu'ils préfèrent dépenser des sommes importantes sur les guerres alors que la moitié du monde meurt de faim.
>
> Thérèse

(*a*) What kind of world would Thérèse like to see in 2038? Mention any **one** thing.

   1

_____

(*b*) Why does she think this is unlikely?

   1

_____

(*c*) According to Thérèse, what are the worst things that governments do? Mention **two** things.

   2

_____

_____

Marks

4. You then read an article about the work of a vet.

VÉTÉRINAIRE

Les vétérinaires s'intéressent bien sûr à la santé des animaux. Certains soignent des animaux domestiques. D'autres travaillent plutôt à la campagne en soignant les animaux de la ferme et d'autres encore s'occupent des animaux sauvages.

Certains vétérinaires font de la recherche en laboratoire, pour trouver des vaccins ou développer des médicaments. Leur travail profite ainsi à l'ensemble des animaux.

Ce qui est évident aussi, c'est qu'un vétérinaire doit aimer les animaux et avoir un très bon sens de l'observation. Un animal ne peut pas expliquer ce qu'il ressent et c'est au vétérinaire donc de savoir faire le diagnostic correct. En plus, il faut aussi être disponible vingt-quatre heures sur vingt-quatre parce que les "patients" peuvent tomber malades à tout moment.

(*a*) We are told that vets work with different groups of animals. Mention any **two** groups.

2

_____

_____

(*b*) What other type of work might a vet do? Mention any **one** thing.

1

_____

(*c*) Why is this type of work important?

1

_____

(*d*) Why does a vet require good powers of observation?

1

_____

(*e*) It takes commitment to be a vet. Explain why this is the case.

1

_____

[Turn over

Marks

5. You read an article about Internet shopping in France.

15 millions de Français achètent en ligne

La France est le pays européen où les utilisateurs d'Internet adoptent le plus vite le commerce électronique.

Entre janvier et mars 2007, 15 millions de personnes ont fait un achat en ligne. C'est 2,5 millions de personnes de plus qu'en 2006. Pourquoi est-ce que les Français aiment de plus en plus acheter sur Internet?

Alors, d'abord c'est vite fait et on peut commander toutes sortes de marchandises sans quitter la maison et à n'importe quelle heure de la journée. Les sites de vente de personne à personne, comme par exemple Ebay, connaissent aussi un grand succès. Sur ces sites la plupart des gens sont honnêtes. Mais certains prennent l'argent pour un "objet vendu" et n'envoient jamais le produit.

Pour éviter ce problème, le gouvernement et les sites ont signé une Charte de Confiance. Ce document fixe des règles pour les échanges entre personnes sur les sites et protège le consommateur.

(*a*) How do recent figures show that French people have taken to Internet shopping? Mention **two** things.　2

_____

_____

(*b*) What are the advantages of buying online? Mention any **two** things.　2

_____

_____

(*c*) What problem can sometimes arise on the "person-to-person" sales sites?　1

_____

(*d*) What is the "Charter of Trust" intended to do? Mention **two** things.　2

_____

_____

Total (26)

[END OF QUESTION PAPER]

C

1000/409

| NATIONAL QUALIFICATIONS 2008 | TUESDAY, 13 MAY 2.30 PM – 3.00 PM (APPROX) | FRENCH STANDARD GRADE Credit Level Listening Transcript |

This paper must not be seen by any candidate.

The material overleaf is provided for use in an emergency only (eg the recording or equipment proving faulty) or where permission has been given in advance by SQA for the material to be read to candidates with additional support needs. The material must be read exactly as printed.

Transcript—Credit Level

Instructions to reader(s):

For each item, read the English **once,** then read the French **three times**, with an interval of 5 seconds between the readings. On completion of the third reading, pause for the length of time indicated in brackets after each item, to allow the candidates to write their answers.

Where special arrangements have been agreed in advance to allow the reading of the material, those sections marked **(f)** should be read by a female speaker and those sections marked **(m)** by a male: those sections marked **(t)** should be read by the teacher.

(t) You are spending a holiday with your family at a campsite in France. One day, you meet André, a French boy who is also on holiday at the campsite.

(m) or (f) **Tu passes des vacances avec ta famille dans un camping en France. Un jour tu rencontres André, un jeune Français qui est aussi en vacances au camping.**

(t) **Question number one.**

André says he saw you at the campsite barbecue last night. Why did he not stay too late? Mention any **one** thing.

(m) **Je t'ai vu au barbecue hier soir. C'était génial, mais j'ai dû me coucher tôt parce que j'étais fatigué après le long voyage.**

(40 seconds)

(t) **Question number two.**

What does André say about his parents? What does he say about eating hamburgers? Mention **two** things.

(m) **A la maison, mes parents sont assez stricts. Je peux manger des hamburgers seulement une fois par semaine. Normalement, je vais au fast-food le vendredi soir avec mes copains.**

(40 seconds)

(t) **Question number three.**

What rules do André's parents have if he goes out during the week? Mention any **one** thing.

(m) **Si je sors dans la semaine je dois rentrer à onze heures et, bien sûr, je dois finir mes devoirs avant de sortir.**

(40 seconds)

(t) **Question number four.**

What does he say about weekends? Mention any **one** thing.

(m) **Le week-end j'ai un peu plus de liberté. Pourtant, je ne vais pas au centre-ville parce que c'est trop dangereux.**

(40 seconds)

(t)   André's family is concerned about the environment.

Question number five.

What does André's father do to protect the environment? Mention any **one** thing.

How else does the family help the environment?

(m)   **Tous les jours mon père va au travail en vélo. En général, il utilise la voiture seulement le week-end.**

En plus, chez nous, nous avons trois poubelles, la poubelle normale et deux autres—une pour les papiers et une pour les bouteilles.

(40 seconds)

(t)   **Question number six.**

André's father is a reporter on the local newspaper.

How does André help him at weekends? Mention **two** things.

(m)   **Mon père est reporter pour le journal de notre ville. Le week-end, je fais des recherches pour lui sur Internet et je téléphone aux gens pour organiser des interviews.**

(40 seconds)

(t)   **Question number seven.**

Why does André like doing this work? Mention **two** things.

(m)   **C'est bien, parce que je gagne de l'argent de poche et quelquefois je rencontre des personnes importantes.**

(40 seconds)

(t)   One evening you hear a radio interview with Sophie Corbin who became famous after winning a singing competition on television.

Question number eight.

Sophie talks about her love of music. What does she say?

(f)   **La musique me passionne. A l'âge de cinq ou six ans, j'ai décidé que je voulais devenir chanteuse professionnelle.**

(40 seconds)

(t)   **Question number nine.**

In what way was Sophie supported at home? Mention **two** things.

(f)   **Mes parents m'ont encouragée tous les deux et c'est ma mère qui m'emmenait aux cours de danse et de musique.**

(40 seconds)

[Turn over for Questions 10 to 14 on *Page four*

(t)   **Question number ten.**

Sophie has a busy lifestyle now. How does she try to stay healthy? Mention any **three** things.

(f)   **Ma vie est très chargée et pour rester en forme j'ai quatre règles. D'abord, il me faut huit heures de sommeil chaque nuit et en plus je mange équilibré. Pour une chanteuse il est nécessaire de protéger sa voix. Donc, je ne fume pas et je bois trois litres d'eau par jour.**

(40 seconds)

(t)   **Question number eleven.**

In what way has Sophie's life changed since she won the competition? Mention any **two** things.

(f)   **Ma vie a complètement changé. Je n'ai plus de problèmes financiers; alors, je porte des vêtements de marque et je loge dans des hôtels de luxe, des hôtels cinq étoiles.**

(40 seconds)

(t)   **Question number twelve.**

She mentions some disadvantages. What does she say? Mention any **two** things.

(f)   **Mais il y a aussi des aspects négatifs . . . par exemple, je n'ai pas beaucoup de temps libre, mes amis me manquent énormément et je ne vois pas souvent mes parents.**

(40 seconds)

(t)   **Question number thirteen.**

Sophie considers herself to be lucky. What does she say? Mention **two** things.

(f)   **J'ai eu de la chance car j'ai déjà visité plusieurs pays et j'ai fait des concerts avec des chanteurs très célèbres.**

(40 seconds)

(t)   **Question number fourteen.**

Sophie goes on to talk about the future. What does she say? Mention any **one** thing.

(f)   **Pour le moment je suis très populaire mais on ne sait jamais si ça va durer longtemps. Beaucoup de jeunes voudraient prendre ma place dans l'avenir.**

(40 seconds)

(t)   **End of test.**

Now look over your answers.

[END OF TRANSCRIPT]

FOR OFFICIAL USE

C

Total Marks

1000/408

NATIONAL
QUALIFICATIONS
2008

TUESDAY, 13 MAY
2.30 PM – 3.00 PM
(APPROX)

**FRENCH
STANDARD GRADE**
Credit Level
Listening

Fill in these boxes and read what is printed below.

Full name of centre

Town

Forename(s)

Surname

Date of birth

Day Month Year

Scottish candidate number

Number of seat

When you are told to do so, open your paper.

You will hear a number of short items in French. You will hear each item three times, then you will have time to write your answer.

Write your answers, **in English**, in this book, in the appropriate spaces.

You may take notes as you are listening to the French, but only in this book.

You may **not** use a French dictionary.

You are not allowed to leave the examination room until the end of the test.

Before leaving the examination room you must give this book to the invigilator. If you do not, you may lose all the marks for this paper.

Marks

You are spending a holiday with your family at a campsite in France. One day, you meet André, a French boy who is also on holiday at the campsite.

Tu passes des vacances avec ta famille dans un camping en France. Un jour tu rencontres André, un jeune Français qui est aussi en vacances au camping.

1. André says he saw you at the campsite barbecue last night. Why did he not stay too late? Mention any **one** thing.

1

_____

*   *   *   *   *

2. (*a*) What does André say about his parents?

1

_____

(*b*) What does he say about eating hamburgers? Mention **two** things.

2

_____

_____

*   *   *   *   *

3. What rules do André's parents have if he goes out during the week? Mention any **one** thing.

1

_____

*   *   *   *   *

4. What does he say about weekends? Mention any **one** thing.

1

_____

*   *   *   *   *

André's family is concerned about the environment.

5. (*a*) What does André's father do to protect the environment? Mention any **one** thing.

1

_____

(*b*) How else does the family help the environment?

1

_____

*   *   *   *   *

Marks

6. André's father is a reporter on the local newspaper. How does André help him at weekends? Mention **two** things.

_____

_____

2

*　　*　　*　　*　　*

7. Why does André like doing this work? Mention **two** things.

_____

_____

2

*　　*　　*　　*　　*

One evening you hear a radio interview with Sophie Corbin who became famous after winning a singing competition on television.

8. Sophie talks about her love of music. What does she say?

_____

1

*　　*　　*　　*　　*

9. In what way was Sophie supported at home? Mention **two** things.

_____

_____

2

*　　*　　*　　*　　*

10. Sophie has a busy lifestyle now. How does she try to stay healthy? Mention any **three** things.

_____

_____

_____

3

*　　*　　*　　*　　*

[Turn over for Questions 11 to 14 on *Page four*

Marks

11. In what way has Sophie's life changed since she won the competition? Mention any **two** things.

2

_____

_____

*   *   *   *   *

12. She mentions some disadvantages. What does she say? Mention any **two** things.

2

_____

_____

*   *   *   *   *

13. Sophie considers herself to be lucky. What does she say? Mention **two** things.

2

_____

_____

*   *   *   *   *

14. Sophie goes on to talk about the future. What does she say? Mention any **one** thing.

1

_____

*   *   *   *   *

Total (25)

[END OF QUESTION PAPER]

STANDARD GRADE | CREDIT

2009

[BLANK PAGE]

FOR OFFICIAL USE

C

Total ☐

1000/403

NATIONAL
QUALIFICATIONS
2009

THURSDAY, 14 MAY
1.30 PM – 2.30 PM

**FRENCH
STANDARD GRADE**
Credit Level
Reading

Fill in these boxes and read what is printed below.

Full name of centre

Town

Forename(s)

Surname

Date of birth
Day　Month　Year

Scottish candidate number

Number of seat

When you are told to do so, open your paper and write your answers **in English** in the spaces provided.

You may use a French dictionary.

Before leaving the examination room you must give this book to the invigilator. If you do not, you may lose all the marks for this paper.

Marks

You are reading a French magazine.

1. On the problem page, there is a letter from Roland who is writing about his father's reaction when he found out that he had his own blog.

RELATIONS DE FAMILLE

J'ai *fait* un blogue mais quand mon père l'a découvert, il était furieux. Il ne me permet plus l'accès à l'ordinateur—ce qui me gêne énormément.   J'ai du mal à faire mes devoirs et je ne peux pas parler avec mes copains sur Internet, donc je me sens très isolé.   Je suis désespéré car mon père ne veut plus en discuter. Que faire?

Roland

(a) In what way has Roland's father punished him?   **1**

He no longer has access to a PC. / not allowed on it.

(b) What effect has this had on Roland? Mention any **one** thing.   **1**

Feels isolated / can't speak to friends online.

(c) Roland is unable to solve this problem. Why?   **1**

His father doesn't want 2 discuss it.

Marks

2. In another article in the magazine, students are discussing after-school classes. You read what Yannis has to say.

> Oui, on peut profiter des cours de soutien dans mon collège. Un grand avantage c'est qu'il y a la possibilité de faire ses devoirs et des profs restent souvent jusqu'à 18h pour nous aider. Comme ça, quand on rentre à la maison, on est libre toute la soirée.
>
>
>
> Ça aide beaucoup car quand on a des difficultés, par exemple en maths, le prof te donne une explication individuelle alors qu'en classe, il explique pour tout le monde! On peut poser toutes les questions qu'on hésite à poser en classe devant les autres élèves, et les profs prennent le temps de tout expliquer cinq ou six fois s'il le faut. Je suis 100% pour!

(a) According to Yannis, what advantages are there in attending these extra classes? Mention any **two** things.

2

_____

_____

(b) What can the teacher do that is different from normal classes?

1

_____

(c) Yannis says that asking questions is easier in these after-school classes. Why? Mention **two** things.

2

_____

_____

[Turn over

Marks

3. You then read Cécile's opinion of these classes.

> Moi je suis contre les cours de soutien après le collège pour les raisons suivantes: souvent on se moque des élèves qui y vont. Par exemple dans mon collège certaines personnes ne parlent pas aux élèves qui vont aux classes supplémentaires! En plus, la journée scolaire est très chargée et on a besoin de se détendre. Un autre problème c'est que ça peut coûter cher car il faut payer le transport à la maison après les classes.

(*a*) Why is Cécile against after-school classes? Mention **two** things.   **2**

_____

_____

(*b*) What other disadvantages are there? Mention any **two** things.   **2**

_____

_____

Marks

4. You read an article about young people taking part in Scout camps.

LES SCOUTS

La vie de scout s'organise par groupes de six ou huit. Les scouts découvrent ainsi la solidarité. Pour le bon déroulement du camp, les tâches sont partagées: préparer les divertissements du soir, s'occuper de la cuisine . . . Ce qui est bien, c'est que les plus grands aident les plus petits à s'intégrer.

Pendant les deux semaines de camp, ça peut être un peu dur de vivre tout le temps les uns avec les autres (surtout sous la tente!). Il n'est pas facile de s'isoler et quelquefois on a envie d'être un peu seul. Cependant, si on a un problème, il y a toujours quelqu'un à qui on peut se confier.

(*a*) Why are the tasks at camp shared out?   1

_____

(*b*) What tasks have to be done at camp? Mention any **one** thing.   1

_____

(*c*) In what way do the older members help?   1

_____

(*d*) Being at camp for two weeks can cause problems. Mention any **one** thing.   1

_____

(*e*) What support is there if someone has a problem?   1

_____

[Turn over

Marks

5. The article goes on to talk about scouts in general.

> Grâce aux activités organisées on apprend plein de choses:
> surtout à respecter les règles et à se débrouiller. En plus, un
> scout donne un coup de main chaque fois qu'il en a l'occasion.
> Il rend services avec le sourire et sans attendre de
> remerciements. Les idées ne manquent pas: déplacer un tas
> de bois, vider un grenier, arroser les jardins . . . les scouts
> sont toujours prêts à aider!

(*a*) The article mentions life skills which scouts learn. What are they?
Mention **two** things.

2

_____

_____

(*b*) Scouts help when they can. What is special about the way they help
others? Mention any **one** thing.

1

_____

(*c*) What kind of tasks might scouts do? Mention any **one** thing.

1

_____

Marks

6. You then read an article about equal rights for men and women.

Les femmes et les hommes ne sont pas payés de la même façon: il y a une différence de salaire moyen d'environ 10% pour exercer le même travail. En plus, certaines femmes font une pause dans leur carrière pour avoir des enfants pendant que leurs collègues masculins continuent à acquérir de l'expérience professionnelle. Le gouvernement a voté une nouvelle loi en mars 2006 pour forcer les entreprises à payer hommes et femmes à égalité. Cette loi prévoit des sanctions pour les entreprises qui ne la respectent pas.

(*a*) Why is the figure of 10% mentioned?

1

_____

(*b*) How are certain women further disadvantaged in their career? Mention **two** things.

2

_____

_____

(*c*) How is a new government law going to help? Mention **two** things.

2

_____

_____

Total (26)

[*END OF QUESTION PAPER*]

[BLANK PAGE]

C

1000/409

NATIONAL
QUALIFICATIONS
2009

THURSDAY, 14 MAY
2.50 PM – 3.20 PM
(APPROX)

FRENCH
STANDARD GRADE
Credit Level
Listening Transcript

This paper must not be seen by any candidate.

The material overleaf is provided for use in an emergency only (eg the recording or equipment proving faulty) or where permission has been given in advance by SQA for the material to be read to candidates with additional support needs. The material must be read exactly as printed.

Transcript—Credit Level

Instructions to reader(s):

For each item, read the English **once,** then read the French **three times**, with an interval of 5 seconds between the readings. On completion of the third reading, pause for the length of time indicated in brackets after each item, to allow the candidates to write their answers.

Where special arrangements have been agreed in advance to allow the reading of the material, those sections marked **(f)** should be read by a female speaker and those marked **(m)** by a male; those sections marked **(t)** should be read by the teacher.

(t)   You listen to Philippe who is working as a French assistant in a Scottish school.

(m) or (f)   **Tu écoutes Philippe qui travaille comme assistant dans un collège écossais.**

(t)   **Question number one.**

Before coming to Scotland Philippe had a job. What did he do?

(m)   **Avant de venir en Ecosse j'ai travaillé dans un office de tourisme tout près de chez moi.**

(40 seconds)

(t)   **Question number two.**

What did he have to do in this job? Mention **two** things.

(m)   **C'était un travail très varié. Par exemple, je devais trouver un logement pour les gens qui visitaient notre région ou bien faire des réservations pour les excursions.**

(40 seconds)

(t)   **Question number three.**

He talks about some of the advantages of the job. What were they? Mention **three** things.

(m)   **Pour moi, il y avait beaucoup d'avantages dans ce job car j'avais l'occasion de parler d'autres langues avec les touristes, je touchais un bon salaire et je ne m'ennuyais jamais!**

(40 seconds)

(t)   **Question number four.**

He then talks about the Scottish school where he is now working. What does he say? Mention any **one** thing.

(m)   **Eh bien, le collège où je travaille est très moderne. Le bâtiment a été construit il y a deux ans seulement.**

(40 seconds)

(t)   **Question number five.**

Why does Philippe think that the pupils in his school are lucky?

(m)   **Les élèves ont de la chance dans ce collège parce que dans la cantine il y a des écrans plasma.**

(*40 seconds*)

(t)   **Question number six.**

He talks about some of the differences between French and Scottish schools.

What does he say? Mention **two** things.

(m)   **J'ai remarqué quelques différences entre les collèges français et écossais. En Ecosse les journées sont beaucoup plus courtes qu'en France et les élèves écossais ont moins de devoirs.**

(*40 seconds*)

(t)   **Question number seven.**

He talks about his pupils. What does he say? Mention any **two** things.

(m)   **En général, je m'entends bien avec les élèves mais je trouve que certains sont très timides et ils ont peur de faire une erreur quand ils parlent français.**

(*40 seconds*)

(t)   **Question number eight.**

He talks about his future career. What does he say? Mention any **one** thing.

(m)   **Ce qui est sûr, c'est que je ne vais pas être professeur parce que je n'ai ni la patience ni l'énergie nécessaire!**

(*40 seconds*)

(t)   **Question number nine.**

One day, you listen to a radio programme for French teenagers. The first interview is with Jean-Pierre, who starts off by talking about "green" issues.

What advice does he give? Mention any **two** things.

(m)   **Tout le monde doit prendre ses responsabilités. Par exemple, on ne doit pas jeter des papiers par terre. En plus, à la maison il faut éteindre la télé quand on n'en a pas besoin. Ce sont des choses très simples mais nécessaires.**

(*40 seconds*)

[Turn over for Questions 10 to 14 on *Page four*

(t)   Question number ten.

He then goes on to talk about the advantages and disadvantages of living in a town.

Mention **one** advantage and **one** disadvantage.

(m)   Il y a bien sûr des avantages à habiter dans une ville. Il y a plein de choses à faire et on a des copains tout près. Par contre, il y a souvent trop de bruit et je ne me sens pas toujours en sécurité si je sors le soir.

(40 seconds)

(t)   Question number eleven.

You then listen to an interview with a famous model, Nadine. She doesn't understand size zero models. Why? Mention **two** things.

(f)   Je ne comprends pas les top-models de taille zéro. Et voilà pourquoi. D'abord, elles ne mangent pas sainement et puis, souvent, elles ne font pas assez d'exercice.

(40 seconds)

(t)   Question number twelve.

Nadine tells you that a model's life can be difficult. What does she say? Mention any **two** things.

(f)   C'est très difficile d'être top-model, ce n'est pas la gloire tout le temps. C'est dur parce que je dois souvent travailler 14 heures par jour, et puis je voyage beaucoup et par conséquent je dors dans un hôtel différent chaque nuit.

(40 seconds)

(t)   Question number thirteen.

Finally you listen to Sylvie who talks about her relationship with her parents. Why does she say her father is too strict? Mention **two** things.

(f)   A mon avis mon père est trop strict. Il dit que je ne dois pas porter de maquillage! En plus, je dois rentrer chez moi avant vingt-deux heures même le week-end. C'est pas normal, ça!

(40 seconds)

(t)   Question number fourteen.

What does she say about her mother? Mention any **two** things.

(f)   Ma mère est vraiment compréhensive et elle a beaucoup de confiance en moi. Je voudrais être exactement comme elle quand j'aurai des enfants.

(40 seconds)

(t)   End of test.

Now look over your answers.

[END OF TRANSCRIPT]

C

FOR OFFICIAL USE

Total Marks

1000/408

NATIONAL
QUALIFICATIONS
2009

THURSDAY, 14 MAY
2.50 PM – 3.20 PM
(APPROX)

**FRENCH
STANDARD GRADE**
Credit Level
Listening

Fill in these boxes and read what is printed below.

Full name of centre

Town

Forename(s)

Surname

Date of birth
　Day　Month　Year　　Scottish candidate number　　Number of seat

When you are told to do so, open your paper.

You will hear a number of short items in French. You will hear each item three times, then you will have time to write your answer.

Write your answers, **in English**, in this book, in the appropriate spaces.

You may take notes as you are listening to the French, but only in this book.

You may **not** use a French dictionary.

You are not allowed to leave the examination room until the end of the test.

Before leaving the examination room you must give this book to the invigilator. If you do not, you may lose all the marks for this paper.

Marks

You listen to Philippe who is working as a French assistant in a Scottish school.

Tu écoutes Philippe qui travaille comme assistant dans un collège écossais.

1. Before coming to Scotland Philippe had a job. What did he do?

_____

1

*　　*　　*　　*　　*

2. What did he have to do in this job?   Mention **two** things.

_____

_____

2

*　　*　　*　　*　　*

3. He talks about some of the advantages of the job. What were they? Mention **three** things.

_____

_____

_____

3

*　　*　　*　　*　　*

4. He then talks about the Scottish school where he is now working. What does he say? Mention any **one** thing.

_____

_____

1

*　　*　　*　　*　　*

5. Why does Philippe think that the pupils in his school are lucky?

_____

_____

1

*　　*　　*　　*　　*

Marks

6. He talks about some of the differences between French and Scottish schools. What does he say? Mention **two** things.

2

In Scotland, _____

_____.

*   *   *   *   *

7. He talks about his pupils. What does he say? Mention any **two** things.

2

_____

_____

*   *   *   *   *

8. He talks about his future career. What does he say? Mention any **one** thing.

1

_____

_____

*   *   *   *   *

9. One day, you listen to a radio programme for French teenagers. The first interview is with Jean-Pierre, who starts off by talking about "green" issues. What advice does he give? Mention any **two** things.

2

_____

_____

*   *   *   *   *

10. He then goes on to talk about the advantages and disadvantages of living in a town. Mention **one** advantage and **one** disadvantage.

2

_____

_____

*   *   *   *   *

[Turn over for Questions 11 to 14 on *Page four*

Marks

11. You then listen to an interview with a famous model, Nadine. She doesn't understand size zero models. Why? Mention **two** things.

2

_____

_____

*   *   *   *   *

12. Nadine tells you that a model's life can be difficult. What does she say? Mention any **two** things.

2

_____

_____

*   *   *   *   *

13. Finally you listen to Sylvie who talks about her relationship with her parents. Why does she say her father is too strict? Mention **two** things.

2

_____

_____

*   *   *   *   *

14. What does she say about her mother? Mention any **two** things.

2

_____

_____

*   *   *   *   *

Total (25)

[END OF QUESTION PAPER]

STANDARD GRADE | CREDIT

2010

[BLANK PAGE]

FOR OFFICIAL USE

C

Total

1000/403

NATIONAL
QUALIFICATIONS
2010

TUESDAY, 11 MAY
1.30 PM – 2.30 PM

**FRENCH
STANDARD GRADE**
Credit Level
Reading

Fill in these boxes and read what is printed below.

Full name of centre

Town

Forename(s)

Surname

Date of birth

Day   Month   Year   Scottish candidate number   Number of seat

When you are told to do so, open your paper and write your answers **in English** in the spaces provided.

You may use a French dictionary.

Before leaving the examination room you must give this book to the Invigilator. If you do not, you may lose all the marks for this paper.

Marks

1. Lucy is writing about her experience with her Spanish pen pal during an exchange visit.

Les correspondants—ce n'est pas toujours facile!

Lorsque ma correspondante espagnole est venue chez moi, ça c'est plutôt mal passé. On l'a reçue pendant une semaine. Immédiatement, j'avais l'impression d'être face à un mur parce que ma correspondante ne faisait aucun effort pour participer à la conversation.

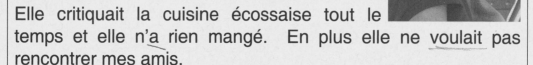

Elle critiquait la cuisine écossaise tout le temps et elle n'a rien mangé. En plus elle ne voulait pas rencontrer mes amis.

Heureusement, je m'entendais bien avec les autres correspondants espagnols. Mais si je peux donner un conseil, je pense qu'il faut avoir un minimum de compétences dans la langue pour faire réussir un échange.

Lucy, 15 ans

(a) Lucy did not get on very well with her pen pal from the start. What does she say? Mention any **three** things.

3

_____

_____

_____

(b) What does Lucy feel is necessary for a successful exchange?

1

_____

Marks

2. You read an article about a security guard.

UN MÉTIER QUI ME PLAÎT

Comme agent de sécurité, je travaille beaucoup avec mon chien. Mon rôle c'est d'empêcher les vols et les dégâts. Je suis responsable de la sécurité d'usines. Mais je suis aussi secouriste et je fais évacuer les personnes en cas d'incendie.

Je connais parfaitement mon animal et j'ai une confiance totale en lui. Je m'entraîne régulièrement avec mon chien parce que nous devons être tous les deux en excellente condition physique!

(*a*) What is his role as a security guard? Mention any **two** things.

2

_____

_____

(*b*) What does he say about his dog? Mention any **two** things.

2

_____

_____

[Turn over

Marks

3. You read an article written by a girl who has just won an award for helping her community.

> Je viens d'une ville au nord de la France qui s'appelle Villeneuve d'Ascq. Avec les autres jeunes de mon quartier et les animateurs du centre de loisirs, nous avons décidé d'organiser une fête l'été dernier. Pourquoi? Eh bien, il y avait une ambiance affreuse dans le quartier: personne ne  se parlait, les gens avaient peur les uns des autres. En plus, beaucoup de parents ne permettaient pas à leurs enfants de jouer dans la rue.

(a) Which **two** groups of people helped her organise the festival?   2

_____

_____

(b) Why did they decide to have a festival? Mention any **three** things.   3

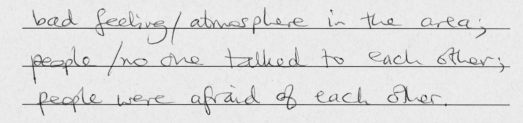

bad feeling / atmosphere in the area;
people / no one talked to each other;
people were afraid of each other.

Marks

4. The article continues.

La fête a été un très grand succès: environ 400 personnes ont participé. Il y avait plein de jeux pour les enfants, mais aussi des parties de cartes pour les plus anciens. Enfin on a  mangé tous ensemble autour d'un barbecue. Maintenant, tout le monde se connaît. On peut mettre un nom sur les visages, on se sourit. L'expérience a été si positive qu'on va refaire une fête chaque année!

(a) What activities were available for the different age groups? Mention **two** things.

2

card games for older people,
lots de games for kids.

(b) What impact has the event had on the community? Mention any **two** things.

2

the experience has been positive,
they want to have a festival every year.

[Turn over

Marks

5. You then read an article about the link between science and sport.

LA SCIENCE AU SERVICE DU SPORT

La France est un pays très sportif et les athlètes français participent au plus haut niveau dans presque tous les sports. Pourtant, la science lutte pour être acceptée dans le sport en France. Certains entraîneurs ont toujours du mal à travailler avec les scientifiques.

Par contre, en Australie, la science dans le sport a déjà commencé à faire la différence. Après l'échec de leurs sportifs aux Jeux Olympiques de 1976, où ils ont gagné seulement cinq médailles, les Australiens ont établi des centres d'entraînement où les sportifs et les scientifiques travaillent ensemble. De nos jours, l'Australie, avec seulement 20 millions d'habitants, est l'un des meilleurs pays du monde sur le plan sportif.

(*a*) What shows that French athletes are already successful? Mention **one** thing.

1

_____

(*b*) What is the relationship between science and sport in France? Mention any **one** thing.

1

_____

(*c*) How did the Australians respond to their poor performance at the 1976 Olympic Games? Mention **one** thing.

1

_____

(*d*) How has Australian sport improved? Mention **one** thing.

1

_____

FRENCH CREDIT READING 2010

1. (a) *Any three from:*
   - It was like she was facing/opposite/talking to a (brick) wall
   - She didn't make any/much/enough effort to/try to/couldn't be bothered to/wouldn't converse/make conversation/wasn't interested in conversing/making conversation
     or
     She wouldn't talk/speak to/with her/them/people
   - She criticised Scottish food/cuisine/cooking/dishes/meals (all the time)
   - She didn't/wouldn't eat (anything)/she had nothing to eat
   - She didn't want to meet/see her friends

   (b) • (Have to have/know) a minimum/basic level of/a bit of (competence/understanding/ability/skill in the) language/some (competence .... in the) language

2. (a) *Any two from:*
   - Prevents/stops theft(s)/robberies/stealing/damage(s)/ vandalism
   - Responsible for (the) factory security/safety/the security/safety of (the) factory/factories
   - He is a first-aider/provides first-aid
   - Evacuates people when there's a fire/in case of fire

   (b) *Any two from:*
   - Knows him perfectly/really well
   - Trusts him completely/totally/has total/complete trust/confidence in him
   - Trains regularly with him/it
   - Has to be in excellent physical shape/condition

3. (a) • Young(er) people/youth(s) from her area/district/community/quarter
      • Leaders/organisers/coordinators from the leisure centre

   (b) *Any three from:*
   - There was a terrible/awful/dreadful/bad atmosphere (in her area)
   - No-one talked (to anyone else/to each other)
     or
     To encourage people to talk to each other
   - People were afraid of one another/others
   - (Lots of) parents didn't allow their children to play in the street

4. (a) • Lots of/plenty games for children/young people
      • Card games/cards for old(er) people

   (b) *Any two from:*
   - Everyone knows everyone else/each other
   - You can put a name to a face/you know people by name
   - People smile at one another/at each other
   - The experience/experiment has been positive/a positive one/a success
   - They are going to do it/have a fête/festival/party/fair every/each year/annually

5. (a) • They take part/perform at the highest/top level (in almost all/most sports)

   (b) *Any one from:*
   - Science struggles to be accepted/fights for acceptance
   - Certain/some coaches/trainers have difficulty/are bad/uncomfortable at/find it difficult working with scientists/science

   (c) • They set up/established training centres where sports people/athletes worked with scientists/sport worked with science

   (d) • It's one of the best/better countries/in the world
      or
      • It's doing better than most other countries

6. (a) • So that they feel less tired/to prevent/fight tiredness/fatigue/to stop them from being/getting/feeling tired
      • To increase muscle power/strength/to build up/pump up muscles/make your muscles bigger
      • To improve/increase (blood) circulation/to make the blood circulate faster

   (b) • Banned/not allowed to enter competition/forbidden from competing/suspended from competition for eight years
      • Had (all) his titles taken away/withdrawn/had to give up/back/gave back/lost his titles

FRENCH CREDIT LISTENING 2010

1. (a) • 12 - 17
   (b) • Every evening/night except Monday

2. *Any two from:*
   • Painting
   • Playing (a musical) instrument(s)/making music
     or
     Musical instruments
   • (Chance to/you can) chat with/talk to friends

3. • A chance to meet in safety/security/it's (a)
     safe/secure (place/environment)
     or
     To be/feel/to keep them safe/secure

4. • Young people/their/the children/they are not
     (hanging about) on the streets/it keeps young
     people off the street
   • Adults (always) there to watch/supervise/keep an
     eye on/look after/take care of their/the children

5. *Any two from:*
   • At the beginning/at first/when it was opened it
     wasn't (very) popular
   • (At the beginning) there were/used to be
     (only/about) 30 members
   • (Usually) 80 (people) go (every evening/now)

6. • There is a good/nice/pleasant/great
     atmosphere/ambience/vibe
   • Activities are organised for everyone

7. • Takes the bin(s)/rubbish out/empties the bin(s) on
     Sunday(s)
   • Watches/babysits/looks after her (little) brother
     after school

8. (a) • Going on holiday with her best friend(s)
         or
         Going (on holiday) to (the) south-west (of)
         France

   (b) • Mobile/phone

9. (a) • Dad is not working/does not work/is
         unemployed/has no job (at the moment)

   (b) • Has a part-time job

10. • Eat (at least) 5 (fruit and veg) per day
    • Don't snack/eat/nibble between meals/no/avoid
      crisps/sweets/sweet things between meals

11. *Any two from:*
    • Take/do regular exercise(s)/exercise often/do
      regular physical activities
    • Walk to school
    • Do things/activities outdoors/outside/in the
      open/fresh air (with friends)

12. *Any two from:*
    • He is very strict
    • He doesn't let her (go)/she's not allowed out
      during the week/on week/school days
    • (He thinks that her) studies are/school
      (work)/education/studying is (very/more)
      important

13. • (She's 15 and) she doesn't have (any)
      freedom/independence/liberty
    • She's not allowed to/can't go to the cinema with (a)
      boy(s)/(her) boyfriend(s)

Hey! I've done it

BrightRED
PUBLISHING

Published by Bright Red Publishing Ltd, 6 Stafford Street, Edinburgh, EH3 7AU
Tel: 0131 220 5804, Fax: 0131 220 6710, enquiries: sales@brightredpublishing.co.uk,
www.brightredpublishing.co.uk

Official SQA answers to 978-1-84948-090-1
2006-2010

SQA STANDARD GRADE CREDIT
FRENCH 2006–2010

FRENCH CREDIT READING
2006

1. (a) • Great/excellent/first rate/cool/top quality fantastic/super/sound/really good/the best/ something else
  • Should/has to/must/ought to try it/give it a try/she should (try to) start smoking/she should do it

  (b) • Won't speak/talk to her (anymore/any longer/again)/will no longer speak to her/will refuse to speak to her/will stop speaking to her

2. (a) • About/approx/almost/nearly half of them/ teenagers/young people/youth(s)/people smoke

  (b) *One from:*
  • More (and more) of them (are beginning to) smoke
  • They start/are smoking younger/ earlier/sooner/they're younger when they start

  (c) *Any two from:*
  • Bad breath
  • Yellow fingers
  • (More) serious illness(es)/diseas(es)/become seriously ill/seriously bad health/disease(s) like cancer…

  (d) *One from:*
  • Refusing to give smokers/smoking a positive image/they refuse to advertise smoking as a positive thing
  • Informing people of the (health) dangers of tobacco/smoking/they give out facts about how bad it is (for your health)

3. (a) • (Amount/weight of) household/domestic waste/rubbish/refuse/garbage/litter

  (b) (i) • Use less packaging/wrapping (like…)
   (ii) • Waste less paper/won't waste too much paper/save (more) paper/paper is going to waste

  (c) • To encourage customers/them/the French/people to buy/use goods which respect/are friendly to the environment/are environmentally friendly/which do not damage the environment
  • Re-use/recycle plastic bags

4. (a) *One from:*
  • He wanted/wants to do something involving/ with sciences/in the field of science(s)
  • He liked/likes/enjoys/enjoyed biochemistry and physics (at school)

  (b) • He studied for 6 years/6 years of study (at college/university)

  or
  He/you finish(es) studying (quite) late
  or
  You don't finish until you are 23 (or older/more)/you need to be (over) 23 (or more) before you start

  (c) • Hospital lab(s)
  • Drug companies/manufacturers of medicines/ drug/medicine manufacturing/places where drugs are made

  (d) *Any two from:*
  • He/one/you has/have to be interested in people
  • He/one/you has/have to get on well with (his) customers/clients/patients
  • They tell him/come to him with/about their health/medical problems
  • He/you explain(s) the/their prescription(s)

5. (a) • Fewer people use the post/less mail/post/ fewer letters/less need for post
  • Less work/fewer jobs for postmen
  or
  Job losses/unemployment for postmen/postmen made redundant

  (b) • Mobile (phone(s)/laptop(s)

  (c) • You/it need(s) chargers and a network/it needs charged and a network/it runs out of batteries and it needs a network

  (d) • Computers do all the work in the future/ computers will do all the work (in the future) for/of men/man/humans
  • People will not become/get/be bored
  • People will be able to give (all) their time/have time to enjoy themselves/have fun/entertain themselves

FRENCH CREDIT LISTENING 2006

1. • We/they get on (well)
   or
   we/they have a good relationship/rapport
   or
   he has a good relationship/rapport with her
   or
   they are (good) friends
   or
   they are (very) close
   or
   she gets on well with him/me

2. *Any two from:*
   • She's on holiday for/we/they (would) (only) spend/spent a/one week here/there/in France/in the hotel/in July/in summer
   • Our/their main/principal/other holiday is/was in winter
     or
     We/they go on holiday in winter

   • We/they spend two weeks/fifteen days skiing
     or
     We/they spend two weeks/fifteen days in Switzerland
     or
     We/they go/went skiing in Switzerland

3. *Any two from:*
   • Lots to do <u>for young(er) people/children/ youth(s)/teenagers/adolescents</u>
   • Theme park
   • (You can go) horse-riding

4. *Any two from:*
   • He's (very) good/gifted/talented (at sport(s)/ it/them)
   • Plays team <u>and</u> individual sports
     or
     He's in (a/the) sports team <u>and</u> does sport on his own
   • (He is/was) school swimming champion
     or
     At school he's (a/the) champion swimmer

5. • Helped/worked in club for/with (young) children/youngsters/kids
     or
     Helped/worked in a club for 5–10 year olds
   • Spent <u>whole</u> day/time/holiday/week/fortnight in the open air/outside/doing outdoor activities

6. (*a*) • Not good/poor/rubbish/no use at/can't do Maths <u>and</u> French

(*b*) *One from:*
   • Not interested in working/sitting in an office/doing office work/sitting behind a desk
     or
     Wouldn't like to/doesn't want to work/sit in an office/do office work/sit behind a desk
   • Must find a job where he'll be active

7. • She read/was enthusiastic about/liked <u>all sorts/kinds of</u> books/lots of <u>different</u> books

   • Sometimes forgot to/didn't/wouldn't come and eat (when/because she was reading/so she could finish her book)
     or
     Sometimes forgot to/didn't/wouldn't eat/forgot mealtimes <u>with the family</u>

8. • Worked/helped/did work experience in local/town/municipal/council library
     or
     worked/helped/did work experience in a/the library in July/in the holidays

   • Replaced the/a librarian (who was on holiday)

9. • To get information from the Internet
   • (Students/pupils/people/they come) to do research/prepare/revise/study <u>for exams</u>

10. (*a*) • He's a farmer/has/had/owns/owned/ran/ works/worked on a (small) farm
      or
      grew/produced/sold fruit/vegetables

    (*b*) • Transported/took produce/products/goods/ stuff/it/fruit/vegetables <u>to market</u> (on Saturday mornings)

11. (*a*) • Treats her like an adult

    (*b*) *One from:*
      • (Too/over) protective when she goes out/wants to go out
      • Doesn't understand/realise that she's no longer a child/that she's a grown up
        or
        He thinks she's <u>still</u> a child

12. *Any two from:*
    • They want to be independent/have independence
    • (They are/can be) influenced by others
    • (They can/could be tempted to) take/be involved in/be offered/do drugs
      or
      (They can/could) drink <u>a lot/too much</u>

13. • They're (very) different (from each other)
    • What they will do (in life/in the future/as a job) does not worry/bother him
      or
      As long as they get a job where they're happy/which they like

FRENCH CREDIT READING 2007

1. (a) She gets <u>more</u> attention (from her parents)

(b) Her parents/they put/there is (a lot of/more) pressure on her about her studies/to study/to do well at school/she is pushed to study

(c) Because you/she/one/they <u>can't/couldn't</u> change anything/the situation/it
it <u>can't</u>/nothing <u>can</u> be changed/it <u>can't</u> change/ you <u>can't</u> do anything about it/ you <u>are/will not be able to</u> change anything/ you can never change it

(d) He has/doesn't lack (lots of) friends <u>at school</u>

(e) He would have to/he wouldn't like to share/divide <u>things/stuff/lots of things/everything/things like</u> (a specific example)
or
he would have to share (<u>two specific examples</u>)

2. (a) Begin to tell/show them/start/teach/educate/train (your child/children/it/them)/do it <u>early/when they are young</u>/do it <u>young/as young/early as possible/at the earliest</u>

(b) • Put (his) teddy/bear/teddy bear on the chair
• Pick/gather <u>up</u>/collect <u>up</u>/(his) toys

(c) Tidy/clean up/clear up your/his/the/their room

(d) The child/tot/toddler/he/she can't/won't/doesn't understand
They don't know what 'tidy your room' means

(e) • Don't leave (your) things on the <u>floor/ground</u>/lying about on the <u>floor</u>
or
Pick your things up off the <u>floor</u>
• Take/bring/put/return (dirty) dishes/glasses/plates <u>to the kitchen</u>

3. (a) Knock before entering (their room)

(b) *Any one from:*
• Their room/it is part of the house/it's not their house/it's their parents' house
• Have to ask parents' permission (to paint room)

(c) There is a risk of going deaf/being deafened/ deafening themselves/losing their hearing/hearing loss

(d) • Vacuum/hoover (their room) <u>every two weeks/fortnight/14/15 days</u>
• Put their (dirty) clothes in the (wash/linen/ laundry) basket
put their laundry in the basket/bin
put their <u>dirty</u> things in the basket/bin
put their things in the <u>wash</u> basket/bin <u>once a week/every week</u>

4. (a) *Any two from:*
• To live in/move/go to a <u>more</u> developed country/countries/somewhere <u>more</u> developed

• <u>To find/for</u> work/a job/employment/to work
• <u>To find/for</u> better living conditions

(b) *Any two from:*
• They may/might not be rich/the richest (countries)/wealthy/they are not necessarily/always rich/richer
• Factories/companies/businesses are (just) setting/starting up/developing/expanding
• They need workers/employees

(c) • They can live/settle/end up/go to/be in areas/regions/places with <u>fewer</u> possibilities of work/with <u>less</u> work.
• There is/has been (already) <u>a lot of/much/ high/a great deal of</u> unemployment

5. (a) Encourage/get/persuade them/people to go (to countries) where they could find/get/be offered work

(b) *Any two from:*
• They have no home/house/residence/(fixed) address/abode/they can't get/will not get a home/they have nowhere to live/ stay/they can't afford a home/they will be homeless
• They have no (work/identity) papers/ID (cards)/documentation/forms/papers
• Return to/go back to/find themselves in poverty/they will be <u>very</u> poor

FRENCH CREDIT LISTENING 2007

1. • Is (very) popular/is (very) busy/is full of people/has lots of people
   • Girls don't pay/girls get in free/it's free for girls

2. • She tells them/says where she is (going)/they know where she is (going)
   • With whom (she's going)/who (she's going) with

3. • She is never/not on her own/alone/she is (always) with someone/people/a group
   or
   She is (always) with a/her friend/(lots of/all her) friends/her friends are/will be with her
   • She has her mobile/phone (in her pocket/on her/with her)

4. (a) She gets on (well)/she has a good relationship with her/they have a good relationship
   or
   Her mother's opinions/attitudes/views/outlook are (very) young/modern
   She sees things in a young/modern way

   (b) (Pocket) money

5. (a) It's not/she doesn't get enough/she'd like to have/she wants/she should have/get/she needs (a bit/little) more

   (b) (She should) find/get/look for/have a job (at the weekend)/she has to/should work (at the weekend)

6. (a) To a holiday village
   or
   To a village in the mountains
   or
   To a village for young people

   (b) Saving (money/up) (a lot)

7. (a) (Rock) climbing
   or
   Pony-trekking/(horse) riding/go on horses/horse trek

   (b) They will discuss plans/projects/ideas/things for the next day/the day after/tomorrow

8. She will be away/on holiday for a (whole/entire) month
   or
   She will be with/meet people/teenagers/ children/kids of her own age

9. *Any two from:*
   • He has been/has been living/has lived/has stayed in Scotland/here/in this country for three years/it's his 3rd year living in Scotland/he moved here three years ago
   • Has/has bought/lives in a new house (there/here)
   or
   Has/has bought/lives in a house in the west/on the west coast/has moved to the west/he lives in the west/a house on the west coast/in the west

   • He has/they have (made) (lots of) (very) good friends (there)

10. • Didn't know anyone/people
    • (Couldn't understand) the/our accent(s)/their accent/couldn't understand the Scots/(Scottish) people/anyone

11. (a) They are from lots of/several/different/other countries/of different nationalities
    or
    They speak lots of/several/different/other foreign languages

    (b) They have to speak (English) slowly/slower

12. (a) (The unpredictability of) the (bad) weather/the climate/the weather is not (always) nice/good/weather changes all the time/weather is unpredictable

    (b) (It's difficult to/you can't (easily)) organise/ organising/plan/arrange outdoor/outside/open air activities/events

13. (a) *Any one from:*
    • They were/the family/he was (quite) poor
    • They lived in a (very) small/tiny flat/apartment
    • They had no car

    (b) *Any one from:*
    • He has no financial/money problems/ worries/he doesn't need to worry about money/he has enough money/lots of money/he is well off/his finances are good/ he is rich/he makes lots of money/finance is not a problem
    • He can see/travel/go all over/tour the world

FRENCH CREDIT READING 2008

1. (a) • She can talk/speak(s)/talks to another/(a) different boy(s)/male(s)/male friend(s)/ lad(s)/guy(s)/boy friend
    • This helps her/she tries to understand the male/masculine mentality/mind/what he is thinking

(b) *Any two from:*
    • They/we are/get/(often) get together/talk/meet/ hang out <u>at break/interval/recess</u>
    • They/we talk <u>about everything/anything</u>
    • They/we <u>go out/go on outings</u> (together) <u>after school/class(es)</u>

(c) • When girls/they are together/in a group they (just) laugh/have a laugh/joke/have fun/mess/fool around
    • (When alone) they have their (own) <u>ideas(s)/ view(s)/opinion(s)</u> on <u>important/serious subjects/things/matters/issues</u>

2. (a) *Any one from:*
    • We/people won't (have/have any/have to) work (any more)
    • Everyone/we will have robots <u>to do their/our jobs/it</u> **or**
    • <u>The work/it</u> will be done by robots **or**
    • Robots will do all the work

(b) *Any two from:*
    • We will <u>travel in/move about in/drive/get around in</u> electric cars/vehicles
    • He/we/people will travel/voyage/journey/go in a flying saucer/go into space
    • He/we/you will talk/speak to extra-terrestrials/ aliens
    • Extra-terrestrials will be his <u>best</u> friends

3. (a) *Any one from:*
    • (All) <u>serious</u> problems (in the world) will have been resolved/there will be no <u>serious</u> problems/(a world) without serious problems
       or
       Solutions/remedies have been found for (all) <u>serious</u> problems
    • No (more) poverty
    • No (more) hunger/famine

(b) (She thinks) <u>governments</u> aren't doing/trying/ helping <u>enough</u>
    or
    Governments aren't (good at) solving/ don't/won't/ can't/are failing to solve (international) problems/the problem

(c) • Governments are spending/wasting/would rather spend (lots of/too much/important/ large sums/amounts of money <u>on war(s)</u>
    • <u>Half the world</u> is starving/hungry/dying of/suffering from hunger/starvation

4. (a) *Any two from:*
    • Pets/domestic/household animals
    • Farm animals
    • Wild animals

(b) *Any one from:*
    • Research in a laboratory/work in a research laboratory/work in laboratory research
    • Finding/looking for/discovering/working on/developing/researching vaccines/ medicines/drugs

(c) *Any one from:*
    • Finding/looking for/discovering/working on/developing/researching vaccines/medicines/drugs
    • It benefits/helps <u>all</u> animals

(d) An animal can't explain/communicate what it is feeling/what is wrong
    or
    The vet must make the right diagnosis/so he can tell what is wrong with the animal

(e) Have to be available/able to work/on call/ready (to work) round the clock/24/7/at all hours
    or
    Patients/animals can fall ill at any time/moment

5. (a) *Any two from:*
    • It's the country where internet shopping is growing at the <u>fastest</u> rate/has taken off <u>fastest</u>
    • 15 million made an online purchase <u>between January and March 2007/in the first 3 months of 2007</u>
    • In 2007 there are/were 2.5 million more internet shoppers than in 2006

(b) *Any two from:*
    • It's fast/quick
    • You can order/buy/get/shop for all sorts of goods/merchandise/products/items/things/ you can get (almost) anything
    • You don't need to leave the house/go out
    • You can order at any time of the day/when you like/24/7

(c) (Some) people (take money but) don't send the/any goods/you don't get/receive the product(s)/goods

(d) • Fix/set rules for buying <u>and</u> selling/ exchanging/trading/exchanges/transactions (on the sites)
    • Protect the consumer/buyer/customer

FRENCH CREDIT LISTENING 2008

1. *Any one from:*
   - He had to go to bed (early)/he went to bed (early)
   - He was tired after the (long) journey/from/after travelling/he had a tiring journey

2. (*a*) (They are (quite/very)) strict

   (*b*) • He <u>can</u> eat/<u>is</u> (only) <u>allowed</u> to eat hamburgers/fast food once a week/one evening/day a week
   - He goes to/eats at a fast food outlet/eats them/hamburgers/it/fast food on <u>Friday</u> (nights/evenings) <u>with his friends</u>

3. *Any one from:*
   - He must be home/in/back by/before/at 11(pm)/he comes/is back by 11
   - He must do/finish his homework <u>before he goes out/</u>first

4. *Any one from:*
   - He has/is given (a little) <u>more/greater/extra</u> freedom/liberty(ies)
   - He doesn't/can't go into the town (centre)
     or
     Town (centre) is (too) dangerous

5. (*a*) *Any one from:*
   - He goes <u>to work</u> by bike (every day)
   - He uses/they use the car at weekends <u>only</u>

   (*b*) They have/use three dustbins/buckets
   or
   They have the normal dustbin and two others
   or
   They have separate dustbins for/they recycle <u>paper and bottles/glass</u>

6. • Gets/looks for information/stories/news (for him) from the internet/researches/does research/looks things up on the internet /he helps his dad by researching on the internet
   • Phones/calls/rings (people) to arrange interviews/he calls people for an interview/he will phone the person who is getting interviewed

7. • He earns/gets his (pocket) money/gets paid
   • He gets to see/he meets/talks to/works with/deals with/is introduced to important/famous people/an important/famous person

8. When she was 5/6 she decided/dreamed of/ wanted to become (a) professional (singer)

9. • Both/the/her <u>parents encouraged</u> her/were <u>encouraging</u>
   • Mother <u>took her/went with her</u> to dance/ music/ singing lessons/classes/courses

10. *Any three from:*
   - Eight hours sleep (per night/day)
   - Balanced diet
   - Doesn't smoke
   - Drinks 3 litres of water <u>per day</u>

11. *Any two from:*
   - No (more) financial/money problem(s)/ worries/cares/issues/financial problems have been resolved/there isn't a money/financial issue any more/now she has no problem with finance
   - Wears/buys/gets/has designer/brand name clothes/ she wears branded labels/logos
   - Stays in/goes to luxury/fancy/de luxe/5 star/posh hotels

12. *Any two from:*
   - Doesn't have a lot of/any/enough free/spare time/time to herself
   - <u>Misses</u> her friends
   - She doesn't see/spend time with her parents/family <u>often/a lot/</u>(as) <u>much</u>/she <u>rarely/hardly</u> sees her parents/family/she doesn't spend <u>much</u> time with her parents/family

13. • She has visited/gets to visit several/many/a number of/lots of/different/other <u>countries</u>
   • She has performed/gets to sing/sung (concerts) with famous singers/she had concerts with….

14. *Any one from:*
   - (She is popular just now but) you don't/she doesn't know how long it's going to last/she might not be popular for long
     or
     She's popular just now but that might change
   - (There are) lots of (young) people (like her who) would like to/ready to take her place

FRENCH CREDIT READING 2009

1. (a) • Doesn't allow him to use/access the computer/he banned/stopped him from using/going on the computer/took away (the use of) his/the computer

   (b) *Any one from:*

   • Difficult to do his homework/can't do his homework <u>easily</u>
   • Can't/doesn't/is not allowed to/won't be able to chat/talk/speak to/communicate with/contact his friends (on the Internet/online)
   • Feels cut off/isolated (from his friends)/lonely/alone

   (c) *Any one from:*
   • Dad <u>won't/doesn't want to/isn't willing to/isn't prepared to</u> discuss (it)/talk/argue (about it)/listen

2. (a) *Any two from:*
   • You can do/get help with/catch up with/finish (your) homework
   • (some) teachers stay <u>until 6/18.00</u> (to give help)
   • You have the (whole) evening(s) free/to yourself/you're free when you go home

   (b) • Teacher explains to individuals/teaches you/speaks to you/works with you/helps you individually/on your own/one to one (rather than to the whole class)/the teacher gives an individual explanation

   (c) • You don't hesitate <u>as you would do in class</u>
   or
   You hesitate <u>in front of others/in class</u>
   or
   You don't have to do it/ask <u>in front of others</u>
   • Teacher can/will explain 5/6/a few/several/many/lots of times/repeatedly/over and over (if needed)/teacher has/can take (more) time to explain

3. (a)/(b) *Any four from:*
   • People/they/we (often) make fun of/mock/laughat/tease the pupils (who go to them)/him/her you get made fun of
   • <u>Some/certain</u> people don't talk to you/those who go
   • School <u>day</u> is (really) busy/hectic/heavy/intense/full
   • Need to/can't relax/unwind/chill (out)
   • Transport (home) can cost a lot/be (too) expensive/you need to pay for transport/to get home

4. (a) • So that the camp/everything runs well/smoothly

   (b) *Any one from:*
   • Organising/preparing (for)/arranging/sorting out <u>evening/night (time)</u> entertainment/activities
   • Cooking/looking after/seeing to/taking care/being in charge of/dealing/helping with the food/kitchen/helping in the kitchen

   (c) • They help the young/younger/youngest members/ones to integrate/fit in/get involved/join in/take part/participate

   (d) *Any one from:*
   • (It's hard/difficult) being/living with others <u>all the time</u>
   • It's not easy to get away from people
   • <u>Sometimes/at times</u> you want to be alone/have time to yourself

   (e) • There's (always) someone to confide in/talk to

5. (a) • Respecting/obeying/following rules/regulations
   • Coping/managing/getting by/surviving/sorting things out (on your own)/being resourceful/fending for yourself/doing things for/by yourself/being independent

   (b) *Any one from:*
   • They (do it with a) smile
   • They don't expect/need thanks/do it without waiting for thanks

   (c) *Any one from:*
   • Shift/move (a pile(s) of) wood
   • Empty/clear out/clean out the attic(s)/loft(s)
   • (Spray) <u>water</u> (on) garden(s)

6. (a) • (10%) salary difference/men get 10% more/women get 10% less <u>for doing the same job</u>

   (b) • They <u>stop work/have a</u> (career) <u>break/take time off/out</u> to have/look after/raise children/a child
   • Male colleagues/men <u>continue to</u> gain/get/build up (professional) experience

   (c) • By <u>forcing businesses/companies/firms</u> to pay/by <u>insisting/demanding that</u> businesses/companies/firms pay men and women equally/the same/all <u>businesses/companies/firms have to</u> give equal pay
   • They will impose sanctions on those which don't (respect/apply the law/it)/businesses will be punished/penalised (if they don't respect/apply the law/it)

FRENCH CREDIT LISTENING 2009

1. • Worked in a tourist/tourism office/tourist information centre/office

2. • Find accommodation/lodgings/hotels/make reservations/bookings for lodgings/hotels (for people/tourists visiting the region)
   or
   Find somewhere to stay <u>for people/ tourists/ visitors</u> (visiting the region)
   • Make/take reservations/bookings for excursions/trips/outings/visits/tours

3. • (Had the chance/opportunity to/could) speak/practise/use other/different/many/lots of languages/another language (with the tourists)
   • (Earned a) good/large/big/o.k salary/wage/pay/was well paid/paid a lot/the money was good
   • (He was) never/not bored/(it was) never/not boring

4. *Any one from:*
   • (The school is very) modern/new
   • (It was) built two years ago/(it is) two years old

5. • The canteen/dining hall has (a) <u>plasma</u> (screen)(s)/TV

6. • Days are/the day is (much) shorter
   • (Pupils/students have/do) less homework

7. *Any two from:*
   • Gets on well with them/they get on well (with each other)
   • (Certain/some) pupils/they are (very) shy/timid
   • They are afraid of making/don't want/like to make <u>a mistake/an error when speaking French/in French</u>/they are afraid of getting/ don't want/like to get it <u>wrong when speaking French/in French</u>

8. *Any one from:*
   • He won't/doesn't want to be/become a teacher
   • He doesn't have the/enough patience/energy <u>to be a teacher</u>

9. *Any two from:*
   • Everyone has to/you/we have to take responsibility/everyone is/you/we are responsible/it's our/your/everyone's responsibility
   • Don't throw (away) paper(s)/litter/rubbish <u>on the ground</u>/don't <u>drop/throw down</u> paper(s)/ litter/rubbish/don't litter
   • Turn/switch off the TV (when not in use/when you don't need it)/don't leave the TV on (standby)

10. *Any one from:*
    • Lots (of things)/more/plenty to do
    • Friends live <u>nearby</u> ·
    and

    Any one from:
    • <u>Too much/a lot of</u> noise/<u>very/too</u> noisy
    • Doesn't (always) feel safe/secure <u>when he goes out/ at night</u>/it's unsafe/not safe <u>when he goes out/at night</u>

11. • They don't eat <u>healthily/sensibly /well/ properly/a balanced diet</u>
    • They don't take/do <u>enough/much/a lot of</u> exercise/they don't exercise <u>often</u>

12. *Any two from:*
    • (Often) has to work/works 14 hours a day/has a 14 hour day
    • Travels a lot/always travelling/on the road
    • Sleeps/stays/lives in a different hotel <u>every night/all the time/regularly</u>

13. • (Tells her) she can't/isn't allowed to/shouldn't wear make-up/he doesn't let her wear make-up
    • Has to be home before/at/by/for 10pm (even) <u>at the weekend/every night/all week</u>

14. *Any two from:*
    • She is understanding/understands her
    • She trusts her/has confidence in her
    • She wants to be (exactly) like her <u>when she has children/in the future</u>

Marks

6. You read another article about athletes who cheat.

Les Sportifs Tricheurs

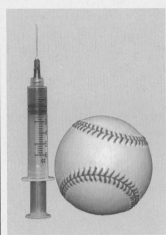

La science est parfois utilisée de façon malhonnête, pour développer les produits dopants*. Certains sportifs les prennent pour moins ressentir la fatigue, pour augmenter la puissance de leurs muscles ou pour améliorer la circulation du sang. Mais ces produits sont interdits. En 2006, Justin Gatlin, le recordman du 100 mètres, a été interdit de toute compétition pendant huit ans et on a retiré tous ses titres sportifs à cause du dopage.

*les produits dopants = banned substances/drugs

(*a*) Why do some sportsmen and women take drugs? Mention **three** things.　　3

_____

_____

_____

(*b*) What penalties did Justin Gatlin receive following his use of banned substances? Mention **two** things.　　2

_____

_____

Total (26)

[END OF QUESTION PAPER]

[BLANK PAGE]

C

1000/409

NATIONAL
QUALIFICATIONS
2010

TUESDAY, 11 MAY
2.50 PM – 3.20 PM
(APPROX)

FRENCH
STANDARD GRADE
Credit Level
Listening Transcript

This paper must not be seen by any candidate.

The material overleaf is provided for use in an emergency only (eg the recording or equipment proving faulty) or where permission has been given in advance by SQA for the material to be read to candidates with additional support needs. The material must be read exactly as printed.

Transcript—Credit Level

Instructions to reader(s):

For each item, read the English **once,** then read the French **three times**, with an interval of 5 seconds between the readings. On completion of the third reading, pause for the length of time indicated in brackets after each item, to allow the candidates to write their answers.

Where special arrangements have been agreed in advance to allow the reading of the material, those sections marked **(f)** should be read by a female speaker and those marked **(m)** by a male; those sections marked **(t)** should be read by the teacher.

(t)   During a stay in France you are listening to the radio. You hear an interview with Christophe Moreau who talks about "Club Jeunesse", the club where he works.

(m) or (f)   **Pendant un séjour en France, tu écoutes la radio. Tu entends une interview avec Christophe Moreau, qui parle du "Club Jeunesse", le club où il travaille.**

(t)   **Question number one.**

What age range does the club cater for? Apart from the weekend, when is it open?

(m)   **Club Jeunesse, c'est pour les jeunes âgés de douze à dix-sept ans. Le club est ouvert le week-end et tous les soirs sauf le lundi.**

(*40 seconds*)

(t)   **Question number two.**

What is on offer for the young people apart from sporting activities? Mention any **two** things.

(m)   **Bien sûr, nous proposons des activités sportives. A part ça, on peut faire de la peinture ou jouer d'un instrument de musique. En plus, on a l'occasion de bavarder avec les copains.**

(*40 seconds*)

(t)   **Question number three.**

For the young people who use the club, why is it important?

(m)   **Le club joue un rôle très important dans la ville car il offre aux jeunes la possibilité de se rencontrer en sécurité.**

(*40 seconds*)

(t)   **Question number four.**

Parents are grateful for what the club offers. Why? Mention **two** things.

(m)   **En plus, les parents sont contents de nos services parce que les jeunes ne traînent pas dans les rues et il y a toujours des adultes pour surveiller leurs enfants.**

(*40 seconds*)

(t) **Question number five.**

What else are we told about the club? Mention any **two** things.

(m) Au début, le club n'était pas vraiment populaire et on comptait seulement trente membres. Mais maintenant il y a en général quatre-vingts jeunes qui viennent chaque soir.

(40 seconds)

(t) **Question number six.**

He tells you why he thinks young people like coming to the club.

What does he say? Mention **two** things.

(m) A mon avis, les ados aiment bien venir au club parce qu'il y a une très bonne ambiance, et surtout parce qu'on organise des activités pour tout le monde.

(40 seconds)

(t) The programme continues with young people phoning in about pocket money.

Question number seven.

What does this girl do to get pocket money? Mention **two** things.

(f) Chez moi, si je veux recevoir de l'argent de poche il y a des choses que je dois faire. Par exemple, je dois sortir la poubelle le dimanche et je garde mon petit frère après le collège.

(40 seconds)

(t) **Question number eight.**

What is she saving for? What does she regularly spend her money on?

(f) En ce moment, je fais des économies pour me permettre de partir en vacances avec ma meilleure amie dans le sud-ouest de la France. L'argent que je reçois m'aide à payer mon portable.

(40 seconds)

(t) The next caller is Marc.

Question number nine.

Why does he not receive pocket money? Why is this not a problem for him?

(m) En ce moment, mon père n'a pas de travail. Il est au chômage. Voilà pourquoi je ne reçois pas d'argent de poche. Mais pour moi, ce n'est pas un gros problème parce que j'ai un petit job à temps partiel.

(40 seconds)

[Turn over for Questions 10 to 13 on *Page four*

(t)   **Question number ten.**

You then listen to a programme about health issues for teenagers. What advice is given on healthy eating?

Mention **two** things.

(m) or (f)   **Bonjour à tous! Comme vous le savez, être en bonne santé est vraiment important et voici quelques conseils:**

D'abord mangez au moins cinq fruits et légumes par jour. Il faut aussi éviter de grignoter entre les repas. Donc, pas de sucreries, pas de chips entre les repas.

(40 seconds)

(t)   **Question number eleven.**

You are now given other tips on staying healthy. What are you told? Mention any **two** things.

(m) or (f)   **En plus il faut pratiquer une activité physique régulière. Ce n'est pas difficile. Vous pouvez aller au collège à pied ou bien faire des activités en plein air avec des copains.**

(40 seconds)

(t)   **Question number twelve.**

The programme also deals with teenage problems. One girl is talking about her father. What does she say about him? Mention any **two** things.

(f)   **Mon père est très sévère. Il ne me laisse pas sortir pendant la semaine. Pour lui, les études sont très importantes.**

(40 seconds)

(t)   **Question number thirteen.**

What else does she find annoying? Mention **two** things.

(f)   **J'ai quinze ans et je n'ai pas de liberté. Ça m'énerve. Par exemple, je n'ai pas la permission d'aller au cinéma avec un garçon! C'est incroyable! Qu'est-ce que je peux faire?**

(40 seconds)

(t)   **End of test.**

Now look over your answers.

[END OF TRANSCRIPT]

FOR OFFICIAL USE

C

Total Mark

1000/408

NATIONAL QUALIFICATIONS 2010

TUESDAY, 11 MAY 2.50 PM – 3.20 PM (APPROX)

FRENCH
STANDARD GRADE
Credit Level
Listening

Fill in these boxes and read what is printed below.

Full name of centre

Town

Forename(s)

Surname

Date of birth

Day   Month   Year   Scottish candidate number   Number of seat

When you are told to do so, open your paper.

You will hear a number of short items in French. You will hear each item three times, then you will have time to write your answer.

Write your answers, **in English**, in this book, in the appropriate spaces.

You may take notes as you are listening to the French, but only in this book.

You may **not** use a French dictionary.

You are not allowed to leave the examination room until the end of the test.

Before leaving the examination room you must give this book to the Invigilator. If you do not, you may lose all the marks for this paper.

Marks

During a stay in France you are listening to the radio. You hear an interview with Christophe Moreau who talks about "Club Jeunesse", the club where he works.

Pendant un séjour en France, tu écoutes la radio. Tu entends une interview avec Christophe Moreau, qui parle du "Club Jeunesse", le club où il travaille.

1. (*a*)   What age range does the club cater for?   1

_____

   (*b*)   Apart from the weekend, when is it open?   1

_____

*   *   *   *   *

2. What is on offer for the young people apart from sporting activities? Mention any **two** things.   2

_____

_____

*   *   *   *   *

3. For the young people who use the club, why is it important?   1

_____

*   *   *   *   *

4. Parents are grateful for what the club offers. Why? Mention **two** things.   2

_____

_____

*   *   *   *   *

5. What else are we told about the club? Mention any **two** things.   2

_____

_____

*   *   *   *   *

Marks

6. He tells you why he thinks young people like coming to the club. What does he say? Mention **two** things.

2

_____

_____

*   *   *   *   *

The programme continues with young people phoning in about pocket money.

7. What does this girl do to get pocket money? Mention **two** things.

2

_____

_____

*   *   *   *   *

8. (*a*) What is she saving for?

1

_____

(*b*) What does she regularly spend her money on?

1

_____

*   *   *   *   *

The next caller is Marc.

9. (*a*) Why does he not receive pocket money?

1

_____

(*b*) Why is this not a problem for him?

1

_____

*   *   *   *   *

10. You then listen to a programme about health issues for teenagers. What advice is given on healthy eating? Mention **two** things.

2

_____

_____

*   *   *   *   *

[Turn over for Questions 11 to 13 on *Page four*

Marks

11. You are now given other tips on staying healthy. What are you told? Mention any **two** things.

2

_____

_____

*   *   *   *   *

12. The programme also deals with teenage problems. One girl is talking about her father. What does she say about him? Mention any **two** things.

2

_____

_____

*   *   *   *   *

13. What else does she find annoying? Mention **two** things.

2

_____

_____

*   *   *   *   *

Total (25)

[END OF QUESTION PAPER]

[BLANK PAGE]

[BLANK PAGE]

[BLANK PAGE]

[BLANK PAGE]

[BLANK PAGE]

[BLANK PAGE]